23. 05. 2012

to Glyn

Read this be
with an open mind
like a child, you already

have gone a long way
Keep searching and you

will find what you

are looking for.

Blessings.

Jan

Without the Light
I Am
Just dust,
With
Eternal Love to
The Father/Mother of All,
The Most High El El Elyon
To YHWH,
To Christ,
To Sophia,
To the Hierarchies of Light.
Thank You

And he said, "Whoever discovers the interpretation of these sayings will not taste death"
Saying 1- Nag Hammadi Scriptures Gospel of Thomas by Marvin Meyer (2007)

A true story of a spiritual awakening

Bring to the Light

Benedetto Daniele Fiorista

Matador
9 Priory Business Park,
Wistow Road, Kibworth Beauchamp,
Leicestershire. LE8 0RX
Tel: (+44) 116 279 2299
Fax: (+44) 116 279 2277
Email: books@troubador.co.uk
Web: www.troubador.co.uk/matador

ISBN 978 1780880 938

British Library Cataloguing in Publication Data.
A catalogue record for this book is available from the British Library.

Printed and bound in the UK by TJ International, Padstow, Cornwall

Matador is an imprint of Troubador Publishing Ltd

Acknowledgements and Gratitude

With love and special thanks to my partner
Because without her I would not have managed to reach the result I needed to reach
to make this book happen.
She has been my teacher and a witness to some of the events.

To the reader
Thank you for finding time to read this book!

I dedicate this book:
To those who are alone and are seeking for the higher truths, because they will find
what they are seeking!
To the ones that are struggling to live between the higher worlds and the lower
world, because they will rest!
To the ones that have faith, because they have the foundation
to reach the Heights.
To the ones that have knowledge,
Because they have been blessed.
And to the ones that have wisdom, because they will know the Glories
of
Our Living God.

"And Jesus said:
The Kingdom is like a person who
Had a treasure hidden in his field and
Did not know it. And when he died, he left it to his son.
The son did not know about it. He took over
The field and sold it. The buyer went plowing,
Discovered the treasure, and began to lend money at
Interest to whom ever he wished."
Saying 109 - Nag Hammadi Scriptures Gospel of Thomas by Marvin Meyer
(2007)

Contents

Preface

I have structured and divided this book into three parts with eleven chapters each, based on the chronological order of events. The first part of the book describes some of the series of metaphysical and paranormal happening, which made me aware of the existences of other realities! These realities were trying to contact me, but at first I struggled to understand any of the meanings and reasons behind matters. This section of the book, shows the process of my awakening and the start of my first Tests, without me actually being aware that I was being put under and such test until a much later stages! I was seeing, sensing and receiving it! I had many experiences with my Soul and Spirit Self, and all I was still working full time at my job.

In the second part of the book, I start to scratch the surface of the meanings of these occurrences as I was developing an understanding of the all, I became more aware of the power of my ego self and his means by which he used to control me and I started to be aware of the battle of the Spiritual Warrior in order to release my soul from the binding control of my lower self. This time I started to invest more time in my spiritual journey and to enable this, I chose to work part-time as I slowly found the right way forward.

The third part of the book is more dedicated to unveiling and understanding of truths and answers through my commitment and studies. I searched constantly for these truths and answers and started calling for my deliverance where through Faith and the help of Humility, Wisdom is reached and through the opening of the gate of Wisdom, Righteousness and Grace shall come forth to abide within us! At this stage I left my job and dedicated my life full time to this journey. All of the events outlined have happened within a time scale of approximately three years.

I have added thirteen drawing of my most significant visions and experiences. These have been roughly sketched by me in order to give a visual stimulation to the reader. Also I have included to meditate on, five pictographic drawings received during my meditations.

The father's kingdom is like a merchant who had a supply
of merchandise and then
found a pearl. That merchant was prudent;
he sold the merchandise and bought the single pearl
for himself.
So also with you, seek his treasure that is unfailing, that is enduring, where no moth
comes to devour and no worm destroys."
Saying 76 - Nag Hammadi Scriptures Gospel of Thomas by Marvin Meyer
(2007).

Introduction

For thousand of years we have heard stories, stories of individuals and communities, we have heard the stories of the Atlanteans, Egyptians, Sumerians, Greeks, Christians, Buddhist, American Indians and Aboriginals and more. Why? I believe, because within these stories that we have been told, there are secrets and these secrets have changed humanity over thousands of years; these secrets are the keys to our evolution!

So let me relate my story of the last three years of my life, this is my true personal experience, the story of a simple individual - but within it lies a message to the world.

It begins from a simple Christian point of view at first as I didn't consider the possibilities of any other spiritual realities. I believed in the existence of God, the only God which is the same God for everyone on Earth. This God is out there and when we die, we shall be judged based on our earthly acts and sent to Heaven or Hell. I had highly simplistic but clear understanding of the Divine but, after a shocking experience, I began to hunger for further knowledge and understanding. I started to look for answers and reasons, which led me to re-read the Holy Bible and uncover some of the codes hidden within it. I found truths in the existences of many realities living a parallel life with us, which at last brought me to find and rediscover The Living God!

I have now devoted over three years of my life to studies, meditations, prayers and experimentations, seeking and revealing ways so that I may succeed in my spiritual guest whilst understanding the true reasons and meanings of my visionary experiences adapting ways to be closer to higher realities.

Some of these visions I saw clearly with my naked eyes, (while I was very sober!) while others I saw after I opened my inner eye a portal through which I started to acquire additional downloads and uplifting energies that brought yet more light and understanding to my experience.

Soon I was lost in the vastness of it all and the fact that, at the beginning of my journey, I didn't know what I was looking for, didn't help. Most of the time I was experiencing things without any clue to the reasons why they were happening to me; but it stimulated me more, made me more determined to find the way and slowly things started being unveiled to me. During this journey I was deceived and misled many times, but this served to give me more strength to try to find the right way. Only by trusting and allowing Higher Guidance into my life was I able to find my answers, to move forward, understand and accomplish what my Spirit-Soul (and later also my Mind) wanted to accomplish while I am in this body, in this life-time. It was all driven by the decoding of my visions, because through them I knew I could find my answers! I felt pressured with fear lurking always barely a breath away from me. Only by remaining open-minded like a child was I able to absorb it all whilst still retaining a firm grip on my earthly reality.

"He Said: these nursing babies are those who enter the kingdom" and then they said to him, "Then shall we enter the kingdom as babies?" Saying 22- Nag Hammadi Scriptures Gospel of Thomas by Marvin Meyer (2007).

There were times when I was elated and times when I was in deep dark places; times where things were clear to me and times where I was in the midst of a thick fog. And times when I thought I was figuring it all out, only to realise that it was merely a tiny particle of later views. I was on my own in this, but in truth I wasn't. I knew it was important to pass on, to reach my goal. Did I find what I was looking for? I let you, reader, decide!

Definitely, I can say that this book reflects in one personal experience the changes prophesied by our ancestors and written about thousands of years ago. I changed - how I look at the world, and the universe beyond - but most importantly I myself changed!

Through these changes, I found the Living God who was being forgotten! He is alive within as well as without. Sure, I changed my habits, comforts and earthly securities, as many of us do. I decided to give the cause my full commitment, investing all of my time and energies to our Creator God, making it the priority in my life and trying my utmost to manifest Love and Light into this world. As I said God became my priority, but the pious or religious one whom many claim to know, but who instead draws us away from what our Living God really wants.

I was being stimulated daily to search for Him in order that He could continue refilling me with knowledge, understanding, Love and Peace not wars, fears and hate. This made me even more respectful of all my surroundings, because the awareness that God is Omni-present in both the visible and the invisible inside all of us, the animal kingdom, the plant kingdom, the mineral kingdom; God is everywhere. He wants us to acquire knowledge and understanding so that we may be granted Wisdom, thus allowing us to indwell with the Heights. It is clear now to me that Faith alone although essential, is not enough.

"For this very reason, make every effort to add to your faith goodness; and to goodness, knowledge; and to knowledge, self-control, and to self control, perseverance; and to perseverance, godliness, and to godliness, brotherly kindness; and to brotherly kindness, love. For if you possess these qualities in increasing measure, they will keep you from being ineffective and unproductive in your knowledge of our Lord Jesus Christ. But if anyone does not have them, he is short-sighted and blind, and has forgotten that he has been cleansed from his past sins." 2 Peter 1:5-9 Holy Bible.

The Dead Sea Scrolls speak about the battle between the children of Light and the children of Darkness. In the revelation of John, he also speaks about the time of the Battle of Armageddon, a battle I believe this battle is very real, I saw it! This battle is active and is happening both within as well as out of us. In my opinion the result of this battle is influenced by the decisions we make inside ourselves on a daily basis which then manifest themselves to our world outside.

We are energy reactors; we produce energies and manifest them in our life through our thoughts, emotions, words, and actions. Because most of us use these forms of energies for self-serving or egoistical purposes and under strong external influences from other means such as television, computers, radios, music, newspapers etc., we are reaching the point of an end! If we don't change our ways, we will have great difficulty adapting ourselves to living within the new time to come! The prophesied heavenly Jerusalem is ready and soon will take place.

Many spiritual books speak about Love, Light and Oneness, which they truly are the keys to this new age. This is the Age of Miracles - an age of transformation. We need to change, evolve and transform ourselves if we want to survive; It is the only way for us to win our battle!

How can we achieve this? By beginning to open our mind and letting things in, rather than creating barriers built with fear and disbelief which serves only to empower our egos that want us to close our minds and not evolve! Sure we do need to use our intellect to discern but in order to discern we need to know what we are discerning!

In the past religions have suppressed higher knowledge with fear and what was not understood or was different was portrayed as evil and put to death. They have tried to alienate higher knowledge or gnosis, destroying valuable books that did not fit within their credo by considering them heretics.

"Many will follow their shameful ways and will bring the way of truth into dispute. In their greed these teachers will exploit you with stories they have made up. Their condemnation has long been hanging over them, and their destruction has not been sleeping." 2 Peter 2:2-3 Holy Bible.

These ancient scriptures were left for us to meditate on in order to understand who we really are, and finally some of them have surfaced for all humanity to access them and ponder on their meanings. These old scriptures - e.g. Codex of Brucianus, Pistis Sophia, Nag Hammadi Scriptures and the Dead Sea Scrolls together with those still lying undiscovered contain great knowledge including our true origins and identity as well as our purpose on Earth; concepts such as soul reincarnation, the presence of other realities and the power of the Light are discussed in detail.

If these scriptures are so important for us, why then have they been hidden from us? And why now why are they easily available to anyone? This is for each one of us to explore and uncover!

It has been said and written, that we are Mind, and it is Mind who directs us; Not our Soul, not our Spirit, but Mind is in control of our actions. It has been said we are the thoughts of God, and what makes a great Mind is knowledge. This means not only the knowledge of our earth science and technologies but really the knowledge which comes with the help of Faith; the true and higher knowledge that comes from far beyond Planet Earth, as indeed do we!

Much knowledge has been channelled through centuries into this planet by higher intelligences and their language of Light has been poured into our consciousness with symbols, rites, names, secret geometry etc. There are now thousands of spiritual courses that include and use these kinds of languages which one can undertake to reach a higher consciousness, but do they work?

Of course, although I believe only we can really change ourselves, through perseverance and daily application of what we have learnt. Never stop seeking because what we are looking for is closer than we think!

"Let one who seeks not stop seeking until one finds. When one finds, one will be troubled. When one is troubled, one will marvel and will reign over all."
Saying 2 - Nag Hammadi Scriptures Gospel of Thomas by Marvin Meyer (2007)

"If the leaders saying to you look the kingdom is in heaven then the birds of heaven will precede you. If they say to you, It is in the sea, then the fish will precede you. Rather, the kingdom is inside you and it is outside you, and when you know yourselves, then you will know, and you will understand that you are a child of the Living Father. But if you don't know yourself then you dwell in poverty and you are poverty". Saying 3 - Nag Hammadi Scriptures Gospel of Thomas by Marvin Meyer (2007).

"But Christ is faithful as a son over God's house. And we are his house, if we hold on to our courage and hope of which we boast." Hebrew 3:6 Holy Bible.

From my personal experience, we must carry on and persist and not give up after receiving our first temporary paranormal experiences, visions and dream experiences that we might receive. Rather we must dig deeper to find the answers.

This requires enormous strength and consistency of will and when we live in a world where our attention is constantly taken up with our daily commitments and responsibilities, it becomes very hard to find the truths that will unbind us.

Blaming the life we live in is not an excuse anymore. The life that each one of us lives is the life that is supposed to teach us to find our true self. For some it is harder than others due to our past life experiences and, of course we have had past lives! It is all about our will, our choices and free will! It is true there are forces that are trying to keep us ignorant and we are deceived every instant of our life time, which is why we need faith and knowledge to acquire the Wisdom enabling us to be granted with higher truths and the ability to recognise the falsehoods. When we have found these truths, then we know who we need to fight against!

We need to acquire the Light, which is this same Light that will transform us. This Light was already part of us but we have been robbed many years ago by these same forces that keep making to stumble and fall. These forces try their best to take the Light away from us and keep us in a state of ignorance and lower earthly consciousness. They are making us believe we are in charge of our present life and future, but in reality we are not; we are puppets!

In one of the parables of Jesus, he spoke about the groom and the brides:

"At that time the kingdom of heaven will be like ten virgins who took their lamps and went out to meet the bridegroom. Five of them were foolish and five wise. The foolish ones took their lamps but did not take any oil with them. The wise, however, took oil in jars along with their lamps. The bridegroom was a long time in coming, and they all became drowsy and fell asleep. At midnight they cry out: 'Here's the

bridegroom! Come out to meet him!' Then all the virgins woke up and trimmed their lamps. The foolish ones said to the wise, 'Give us some of your oil; our lamps are going out'. 'No,' they replied, there may not be enough for both us and you, instead go to those who sell oil and buy some for yourselves'. But while they were on their way to buy the oil, the bridegroom arrived. The virgins who were ready went in with him to the wedding banquet. And the door was shut. Later the others also came. 'Sir! Sir!' they said. 'Open the door for us!' But he replied, 'I tell you the truth, I don't know you'! Therefore keep watch, because you do not know the day or the hour. " Matthew 25:1-13

Time is running out. We need to master ourselves and unite together for the good of all of us. I believe everyone has the ability to create, but what can we create, if we are tossed and battered like small boats on a stormy sea? And the more we are battered, the more we shall be. Only through raising our consciousness and letting go of the things that are holding us back in the storm, can we rise up and experience the blessing that our Father God has given to us with love. Only through the process of monitoring and transmuting can we see the Light within and without.

"This heaven will pass away and the one above it will pass away, The dead are not alive, and the living will not die. During the days when you ate what is dead, you made it alive. When you are in the light, what will you do? On the day when you were one, you become two, but when you became two, what will you do?"
Saying 11 - Nag Hammadi Scriptures Gospel of Thomas by Marvin Meyer
(2007).

What I write in this book is the truth. I am not trying to sell you anything, but what I have been told to do is to bring to the light what has been given to me.

"What you hear in your ear, in the other ear proclaim it from your rooftops, For no one lights a lamp and puts it under a basket, nor does one put it in a hidden place. Rather, one puts it on the stand so that all who come and go will see its light".

Saying 33 - Nag Hammadi Scriptures Gospel of Thomas by Marvin Meyer (2007).

I hope with all my heart that this book finds you and sheds light into your consciousness, that my words and experiences will deliver you some answers. We are evolving as a species but most of us don't see or hear it. Maybe we are too busy with our lives and problems or maybe like Saint Thomas, if we don't see and hear it, we don't believe it! Either way, choices are truly ours. Remember the Light is always there waiting for us to be acknowledged and discovered, and when we find the Light, we really start to know who we are and what YHWH has reserved for us!

Part One

Prayer of the Apostle Paul★

Oh Father of all Fatherhoods, Unending Light
limitless, Unfathomable, Immeasurable,
Invisible, Eternal, Unutterable
Unnameable, Un-generated and Self Generated One.
Grant me your mercy.
My Redeemer, redeem me, for I am yours;
I have come from you.
You are Mind:
Bring me forth.
You are my treasury:
Open for me.
You are my Fullness:
Accept me
You are my rest:
Give me incomprehensible perfection.
I call upon you
You who exist and preexisted,
ATIK YOMIN
In the name exalted above every name,
YHWH
Through Jesus Christ,
Lord of Lords
ADONAI HA ADONIM,
King of the eternal realms
MELECK SH'MAYA.
Give me your gifts, with no regret,
Through the Son of Humanity,
The spirit,
The advocate of truth
KAVOD CHRISTOU,

Give me authority, I ask you,
Give healing for my body, since I ask you
Through the preacher of the gospel,
And redeem my eternal enlightened soul and my spirit,
And disclose to my mind the firstborn of the fullness of grace.
Grant what eyes of angels have not seen,
What ears of the rulers have not heard,
And what has not arisen in the human heart,
Which became angelic,
Made in the image of the animated God
When it was formed in the beginning.
I have faith and hope
And bestow upon me your beloved, chosen, blessed majesty,
The firstborn, the first begotten
The wonderful mystery of your house.
For yours is power and glory
And praise and greatness
Forever and ever.
Amen

★This prayer was found in the Nag Hammadi Scripture edition 2007 page 17-18 by Marvin Meyer, but the first part of the prayer is missing, it has been lost, so I have added parts to complete the parts missing taken from the book The Secret Book of John from the same book. I have also added Sacred Names, where I felt was needed.

Chapter 1

About Myself

I was born in Sicily, Italy. My parents are Catholics but I did not have a strong religious background although I was baptised and I took my first communion. When in my early twenties I first started to read some of the books which contained Eastern thought influences and I found in them wisdom and different ways of how to view the world. My only experience of Western spirituality came from reading a Bible which had been given to me as a gift before I left Sicily to work abroad. I read my Bible only once several months later but I always took it with me as a good luck talisman whenever I travelled. I found that it helped me to keep in mind that there was always somebody out there looking after me and making sure I was doing the right thing. I always believed there was only one God. I gave my Bible to my brother a few years ago, when he asked me if he could read it, and since then I decided to leave it with him. I was no longer interested in conventional religions as I viewed them full of pride, hypocrisy and aggression – needing to control and being highly judgemental. I was more interested in living and learning through my daily experiences and exchanging thoughts with people of different backgrounds and philosophies. I thought this approach would best serve me to became wiser in my old age, bringing me peace and self confidence in life, knowing that I would have lived my life fully.

My first experience with "New Age" spiritual thinking was in the beginning of 1997 on a Maldivian island where I was working as a diving instructor. One of my clients heard that I had some discomfort in the area of my middle back towards the centre of my spine. He told his wife to give me a healing. At first I was uncomfortable and sceptical but I wanted to be polite and so agreed. I was outside by the beach restaurant at the time but she assured me that I did not need to move; she could work by only putting her hands on my shoulders, which she did. While she stood behind me with her hands placed on my shoulders I started to feel the sensation of warmth gently concentrated on the affected area, making my pain lessen and slowly disappear. This was my first experience of a Reiki healing.

I met my partner while I was working in the Maldives and together we worked on a wonderful project which consisted of living on a boat mapping dive sites around the atolls of the Maldivian islands. This was at the beginning of 2000, but, when the project ended a few months later I found myself living in Wales, where I have spent most of the last 12 years. It was here that I reconnected with Reiki becoming a Ursui Master Teacher in 2007. I enjoyed the experience and although I never felt entirely comfortable at the thought of being seen by others as something of a magician! I did my best to keep my mind open, soon I acknowledged the feeling and the presence of energy fields around and through my hands, which were generating heat. I did not perform many healings on other people but I was mainly channeling it to myself before falling asleep in bed. It was very relaxing.

My experimentation with Reiki stopped when I was trying to clear a place in France from negative energies and I realised I was doing it from the point of ego and thus I was completely unprotected and unprepared, for what I encountered. As result of this I ended up in hospital for nearly a week, unable to eat and drink, with a fever of 40+C. Before opting to go to the hospital, I had been trying to heal myself, but I had been getting worse and worse each time! Only when I was in the hospital and I believed that I was being looked after by Angels, with compassion and love. I did feel safe once more.

After this experience I honestly did not want to ever try Reiki or any other spiritual experience again but I also learnt to never say never!

Chapter 2

The Beginning of the Change
– The Cottage

In the winter of 2008 my partner and I decided to live apart for a few months so I rented a cottage. The cottage was beautiful situated only two miles away from where I was living and, being surrounded by open fields, it was not only peaceful and relaxing but also an ideal environment for walking my dogs in the morning before I left for work and again in the afternoon when I returned home.

Although I was oblivious to it at the time, renting this property would prove to be a pivotal event in my life and the key to my spiritual awakening. It all began with how it made me feel at night. Initially, I thought it was because it was so isolated and very dark that it made me feel unsafe, but then I found I simply could not sleep in the night. I knew there were invasive energies trying to approach me and sensed something watching me all the time. More than once in the middle of the night when I opened my eyes I could see a ball of white/reddish light around me, flashing away, sometimes in my face, which I found very disturbing. My dogs, sometimes with no apparent reason, would start barking and getting very unsettled. So I began checking outside but found nothing – it was silent everywhere. I thought that perhaps the cottage was haunted by a lost ghost, a spirit or an entity that was trying to scare me, but because of my life situation at that time, I could not care less about spirit activities. I was letting go of lots of things within me. I spoke to my partner about this, and when she stayed with me a couple of nights she agreed with me. This didn't stop me sleeping there, when I felt the need to have more space for myself and I often chose to return have to sleep on my own without understand why.

Most nights, as soon as I was standing in front of the main door, I felt a strong pressure and even a pain in the back of my head, making my hair rise up. I knew that my unseen friends were there, waiting for me. One day I was talking with the landlord of the cottage, who had refurbished the cottage from an old derelict ruin, and I was trying to get some feedback from him regarding unseen entities. He had lived in the cottage for a while, before he started to rent it out. So I was intrigued to hear from him but he told me that only inexplicable experience he could recall was when one of his holidaying guests had started screaming in the middle of the night and left the place hurriedly. This happened when she was on her own, after her husband was spending a night in the local hospital. He looked in my eyes and said, with an ironic tone, "Maybe there are ghosts here" quickly adding that the remoteness of the cottage probably scared people. Of course, I did not agree with this statement, but I kept my sentiment to myself.

Chapter 3

The Awakening

In January 2009 I was still living in the cottage, with the usual spirit disturbances occurring. One day, I was invited to join a spiritual course called Munay Ki because somebody else was supposed to go instead but couldn't make it. I did not have a clue what it was about, except that I remember she told me that it embraced masculine energies, and that I would like it. As my curiosity had been raised by the activity at the cottage, I accepted and, on the 23rd of January 2009 attended the course.

I remember our Munay Ki rites giver was meticulous woman and she had prepared everything for the day, plus she had a small stock of all sorts of spiritual items. After the initial introductions, all four of us then sat on the floor around a little altar, with cards of animals pointing outward, in each of the four directions of the cardinal points. I was sitting in the South position which was the place of the snake, so the card of a snake was in front of me. To the West there was a Jaguar; the North a Humming bird and the East the Eagle, plus there were some other cards that, she told us, were representing Pachacuti; Huascar, Mother Earth and other figures all there circling a plate with a candle. She carefully explained the origin of Munay Ki and the significance of the cards. From the South American Shamans it was introduced to the west by a Cuban/American called Alberto Villoldo who spent many years studying under some of the Shamans of Peru. As a result of this he later brought these Rites of Munay Ki to the USA and Europe.

We started by opening a Sacred Place together by calling the spirits from each direction before picking a card from a beautifully illustrated deck called *Medicine Card by Jamie Sams & David Carson*, complete and well explained text based upon American Indian wisdom. Everyone took their card and my card was a coyote. On reading it, I thought it was not a very nice card as it implied to me was that something significant was going to happen to me as a result of me taking things too lightly. This resonated in me intensely, because I associated it with my late experiences in the cottage. I felt that something or somebody was warning me. While I was reading my card of the coyote aloud the other participants were laughing about the interpretation, but I was not.

I put the card episode behind me and carried on with the day. Finally, we received our first four rites which were called the Rites of Initiation. Everyone else saw colours and were aware of beautiful feelings, but I did not feel or see anything! The tutor gave us handouts to read at our leisure and instructed us we were supposed to feed our rites daily using a candle for at least 21 days, I was adamant that there was no possibility that I would spent an hour a day for the next three weeks doing that and in a rush, we finished our day although I did buy a couple of books before we left as she was such a pleasant, kind soul.

I decided to spend the rest of the week in the cottage with two of my dogs. On that Saturday night while I was cooking I was looking at a Munay Ki handout and video, given to me on the course, which contained testimonials of people about their experiences with Munay Ki. I found it reasonably interesting, it showed how to feed the rites with the flame of a candle.

That night, I went to bed about 11pm and suffered a series of strange events – lights going off and then coming back on again, dogs barking for no reason – which intensified during the night. I remember I didn't want to sleep but just lay in bed with the light on until 1am before switching it off and trying to sleep. I felt pressured and uncomfortable but I believe I did fall asleep after a while - and it was then when things started to happen in earnest. I had a clear vision, not a dream but a clear vision while I was fully aware of my senses. A strong image of the card snake appeared to me, shocking me and making me jump out of bed and turn the side light on again. After a few minutes, I convinced myself I was just tired so I turned the bedside light off again and I close my eyes only to have the word Huascar (Lord of the Underworld) spring into my mind, together with the image of an angry American Indian in black and white. I believed it was Huascar – somebody or something was warning me!

While still I was fully aware of what was happening, I felt my body shrinking. When I tried to wake up I had to fight very hard to have a response from my body. Before that, I remember reading a text on my mobile that had just arrived from my partner asking, 'Are you OK?' I thought this was at about 1.30am, but later when actually I spoke with her at around 7am I learned she sent it at 3.45am as she had woken up suddenly feeling concerned about me - the time I was experiencing all these strange events! From 4.15 to around 5am I lay watching the ceiling with the light on, observing movement near the centre of the ceiling, before thinking it was the time to get up and get out of there. I had a shower then breakfast and I tried to make some sense of what was happening to me. Was it just my imagination? Was I over-tired? Was it a bad dream? Was I going mad? I was more shocked than scared. I became more cautions and took things more seriously, including trying to protect myself. I didn't want to wake my partner and scare her so early in the morning so I opted to wait until about 7am before ringing.

While, I was waiting, I noticed on the table there were the animal cards and the book I had bought a couple days earlier during the Munay Ki course. I was curious about the meaning of the snake. I was sure I had not dreamt the vision, so I started to read about the snake, which turned out to be a sign of an imminent change!

I was exhausted; as I had had almost no sleep. Finally, I rang my partner and after talking things over I decided that it was a good idea for me to leave the cottage immediately and to go to rest at her house.

On arrival, I related the happenings of the past night. She reiterated that she had sent the message at 3.45am whereas for me it was only 1.30am on my watch when I had read it. I was so sure about it, it appeared to me as if time was going forwards and backwards. To my relief, I was finally in bed and sleep came easily.

Little was I to know but this was only the beginning! For four days I didn't sleep yet I didn't even feel tired or the need to sleep. The incredible events that unfolded over these next four days were to change my life irrevocably and forever.

I awoke with a bit of sore throat and a slightly high temperature, so I rested in bed for most of the day. Just as well as, the night time. and it was in the night time I began to see and feel happenings way beyond my wildest imagination, commencing with me perceiving a tumultuous spiral of swivelling energies which gradually gained colour developing forms and shapes. I was aware of being stared at by grotesques series of red eyes and shiny black eyes lined up at the bottom of my bed. Surely I was hallucinating, I thought but my partner witnessed them too. I was desperately trying to protect myself by surrounding myself with white Light and calling on Archangel Michael and Jesus, to keep all evil away from me. No matter how hard I tried I could not hold them back and the effort made me perspire profusely, soaking the bed with sweat.

In the midst all of this turmoil and red eyes, I started to have a vision. I was flying to places I had never been before and flying very fast before entering a dark tunnel or well, rising up and up until I emerged in the middle of a gathering of some Peruvian Shamans sat praying in a semicircular formation. From there, I flew off high above the mountains and I went to visit other places before I realised I was returning to my physical body. I really could not understand what had happened – had my soul left my body? When I re-entered my body I found I was still sweating and trying to keep all the entities or spirits safely away from me. I could see these grotesque figures at the foot of my bed and I was feeling immense pressure that I could not manage. The atmosphere in the room was extremely tense for me. I took my boji stones (2 small stones, which help to ground energies to Mother Earth) and placed one in each hand, which slowly helped me to ground and drain all this turmoil from the room. These energies were coursing through me and I gradually I discovered that channelling these energies down through my feet was improving the atmosphere. The pressure started to ease and I was able to relax a little. I contemplated the situation and recognised that if I could not fight them off, I should attempt to channel their energy and ground it to Mother Earth and this helped to clear the room of spirits - but only temporarily!

The respite did not last for long, however, but I was fully aware of the other beings crowding into my bedroom except they were no longer faded figures but rather clean images visible to my naked eye. Aliens! – Appearing similar to Dark Vader of the 'Star Wars' films, with metallic faces wearing mask-helmets and short in stature, quickly followed by others of odd and grotesque forms. I could not establish if there were coming to do me harm, or if they were coming to protect me. Although their behaviour was more of curiosity than of posing threat. Next there appeared a great multi-coloured circle with the brightest blue, green, yellow, orange and red I had ever seen in all my life. I had never seen colours so vividly beautiful, not just bright; but also so pure, so clean – and in the midst of this colours I saw a beautiful Being of Light almost ghost-like but not a ghost flying towards me. As I was admiring this Being of Light so I spotted another similar one below him but this time it was a Child coming to me.

My confidence grew so the following night I started to be inquisitive: could I see my Guardian Angels? Were there any messages for me? The possibilities seemed endless. I started to close my eyes while holding my boji stones in my hands, because I was still seeing gloomy grotesques figures with their red eyes around me at times as well as animals spirits and aliens. I was still sweating profusely and needing to change my pyjamas two or three time a night. I witnessed many things during these four days – animal spirits, persistent aliens and one night, the vivid figure of an open winged Eagle formed on my pillow, made of my own sweat with every detail; delicate depicted like a fine art drawing no imagination was necessary!

After the forth day the activity started to calm down, and in someways I was disappointed as I had become very eager to see what was coming. Physically I felt excellent, my spine felt like a piece of steel and I was elated and had the sensation of invincibility.

"Where there are three Deities, they are divine, where there are two or One, I am with that one!"
Saying 30 – Nag Hammadi Scriptures Gospel of Thomas by Marvin Meyer (2007).

"But everything exposed by the light becomes visible, for it is light that makes everything visible. This is why it is said:
'Wake up, O sleeper,
Rise from the dead,
And Christ will shine on you'."
Ephesians 5:13-14 Holy Bible

"This is the covenant I will make with the house of Israel,
After that time, says the Lord.
I will put my laws in their hearts,
And I will write them in their
Mind.
I will be their God,
And they will be my people.
No longer will a man teach his neighbour, or a man his brother,
Saying, 'know the Lord'
Because they will all know me, from the least of them to the greatest'. For I will
forgive their wickedness and will remember their sins no more."
Jeremy 31:33-34 Holy Bible

Life on Earth, with all its daily stresses worries, and happenings, now seemed so remote. I felt untouchable, removed in every sense, as if my past was gone, and I was a new person.

By the Fifth day events seemed more under control, so I perceived now it was a good idea to spend a little time each day feeding my rites through the chakras, and I considered doing it at night before I went to bed to be the best time. Nervously at first as I was unsure as to my actions, I started to perform my ceremonies to open my sacred place, initially spending around 30 minutes to complete the task. I felt it was imperative to feed my rites every night without fail. I did this by invoking the Four Directions, the Archetypes above and Mother Earth below together with Great Spirit and then, sitting in the lotus position in front of a candle, I took in the light from the candle with my hands to feed my chakras (a Shamanic way to feed the chakras). During these days, I was trying to get some feedback from people who have done this Munay Ki course before in order to understand what was happening to me. Were these common reactions? Did others have similar reactions of mine? I rang the Munay Ki rites giver and related my story to her, and she assured me it was quite normal and that after a few days everything will calm down. I was very surprised by her answers; as I knew within me that it could not be normal but that something very, very special was happening to me. I could not let it pass lightly and I felt very strongly that I needed to find out what had really happened but now I understood that I was going to explore it by myself and so I started independent my studies. The first book I selected to read was one bought at her shop: *Shaman Healer Sage by Dr Alberto Villoldo (2000)*

I will always remember those following months as I started to have meaningful visions and dreams. That bore witness to my consciousness of other existences. These visions stimulated me further giving me the strength and courage to pursue the real truths.

My first couple of meaningful visions or dreams I had subsequent to those first shocking appearances follow below.

In my first vision or dream: I saw a tall beautiful woman, standing in my hallway in front of the door ready to leave. When I saw her I rose from my bed and went towards her and I asked if she was okay. She turned to me with her beautiful eyes, saying she was fine, and that she only wanted to see me, because she had been feeling my energy and she wanted to see with her own eyes. Then, in a fraction of a second, I turned my head and she disappeared, and instead I saw one of my dogs, looking at me with his gentle eyes. He was outside in the garden and I was watching him from the window.

The second dream or vision was as follows: *I saw a tall man who I recognized a farmer or an owner of the land close to my house. Resemblances are nothing to do with real appearance. When I saw him approaching the house in an aggressive mode I went to see him in the garden, I met him nearby to the old oak tree in front the house. He told me that he was keeping a close eye on me, observing my every move, and he told me, he will be very hard on me if I don't take serious enough his warnings. At first I didn't know what to think, and then I thought maybe he was speaking about his land, because I go there with my dogs every day, sometimes twice a day. Perhaps he was implying that I was showing no respect for his land, surely this was not the case, I was asking him why I would not be respectful? What had I done to be approached in this way? So I start to chat with him; I invited him into the house while I was preparing my breakfast. As I was heating my milk it went bad with black spots in it, and I had to throw it away. I was doing my best to be friendly but I could see he was watching me disapprovingly, and was not interested to hear what I had to say. Then in his way out, I saw all his animals – cows, goats and sheep – in the garden and suddenly it started to rain very hard, with hailstones, so I told him to wait until the downpour was over, and I remembered my dogs were out too, so I started to call them in. Two of the five dogs came into the conservatory but I was slow to close the door and a goat and a little lamb followed them. Then they went on into the house together with the two dogs and I was watching them just in case one of my dogs would attack them. But I noticed the lamb was lying happily with one of my dogs, and when I turned to remark on this to the farmer he told me to be careful with the other dog as she is more insecure After looking at the other dog, I turned towards the farmer and he was not there anymore.*

These dreams stayed with me; the first one I saw as a welcoming and loving, and the second I saw as anger and a threat.

"They are like children living in a field that is not theirs. When the owners of the field come, they will say, 'Give our field back to us'. They take off their clothes in front of them in order to give it back to them.
For this reason I say, if the owner of the house knows that a thief is coming, he will be on guard before the thief arrives and will not let the thief break into the house of his estate and steal his possessions. As for you, then, be on guard against the world. Arm yourselves with great strength, or the robbers might find a way to get to you, for the trouble you expect will come. Let there be among you a person who understands.
When the crop is ripened, the person came quickly with sickle in hand harvested it. whoever has ear to hear should hear."
Saying 21 – Nag Hammadi Scriptures Gospel of Thomas by Marvin Meyer (2007).

It was more than two years, before I could understand the meanings of these dreams.

Hymn of the Saviour

Now I, the perfect forethought of the All, transformed myself into my off-spring. I existed first and went down every path.

I am the abundance of light,
I am the remembrance of the Fullness.

I travelled in the realm of great darkness, and continued until I entered the midst of the prison. The foundations of chaos shook, and I hid from them because of their evil, and they did not recognize me.
Again I returned, a second time, and went on. I had come from the inhabitants of light, - I, the remembrance of Forethought.

I entered the midst of darkness and bowels of the underworld, turning to my task. The foundation of chaos shook as though to fall upon those who dwell in chaos and destroy them. Again I hurried back to the root of my light so they might not be destroyed before their time.
Again, a third time, I went forth

I am the light dwelling in the light,
I am the remembrance of forethought

So that I might enter the midst of darkness and the bowels of the underworld, I brightened my face with light from the consummation of their realm and entered the midst of their prison, which is the prison of the body.
I said, Let whoever hears arise from the deep sleep.
A person wept and shed tears. Bitter tears the person wiped away, and said, 'Who is calling my name? From where has my hope come as I dwell in the bondage of prison?'
I said,
I am the forethought of pure light,

I am the thought of the Virgin Spirit, who raises you to a place of honour.
Arise, remember that you have heard
And trace your root,
Which is - I , the compassionate.
Guard yourself against the angels of misery,
The demons of chaos, and all who entrap you
And be aware of the deep sleep
And the trap in the bowels of the underworld.
I raised and sealed the person in luminous water with Five Seals that death
might not prevail over the person from that moment on.
Page. 131-132 The secret book of John Nag Hammadi Scriptures by Mar-
vin Meyer (2007).

Chapter 4

The Opening of My Inner Eye

After a suitable interval I attended the second out of the three courses that make up the Munay Ki. This time I chose to go to another healer, as she was passing the next rites over a two day period, which I considered would be more relaxing and enjoyable. The workshop was held in a beautiful old mill by a gently flowing river, a all in all very peaceful location. After only fifteen minutes of driving I started to feel the first pressure on my forehead. Initially intermittent, with very strong pressure resembling somebody pushing in an area of about 20 cm diameter at the middle of my forehead. At first I thought it was a premonition, but then, after another ten minutes, the pressure was released and nothing had happened. I thought this was very strange, as the same had happened a couple of times during the past week, although, at the time, I had attributed it to the intensity and pressures of the energies my body was experiencing, pushing my brain to the absolute limit. I also noticed that every time this pressure was coming, it was increasingly intense.

The new Munay Ki teacher, I thought, was very professional a simultaneously strong willed. The atmosphere was comfortable and she was very well organised giving an introductory briefing outlining the programme. We opened our directions together by invoking the Archetypes and Archangels, before holding a meditation session as she prepared us to receive the next two rites.

The most memorable thing that I felt during this ritual was when I received the Rite of the Daykeepers into my sacral chakra.It was an overwhelmingly powerful shot of energies that left me out of breath. After receiving both rites I felt extremely drained and, once home I sowered and collapsed into bed.

On the second day we promptly shared our experiences of the day before repeating the initial steps of opening the directions and holding a meditation session to relax.As the meditation started I once again began to feel that same strange pressure on my forehead and began seeing more I again saw beings and colours. For me, I was discovering the unknown and the unknown was stimulating me more. I was amazed what could be seen using visualizations techniques although I did not fully comprehend what I was seeing.

On this day gave us only one rite, that of the Earthkeeper, but it was intense, I had the sensation of fire shooting through my crown chakra, I experienced lights and colours mainly pink then I saw colours, this was followed by what seemed to be a placenta I could see all the thin blood vessels surrounding it, inside this placenta I saw a bright white ball of Light that transformed itself into a big strong Angel who flew towards me.

We were finished by mid-day so we went for a stroll along the stream. The rites giver suggested feeding our rites along the stream, so we could feel the energies around us and attune with them. While walking, our tutor told us that the day before, she had spotted a lost sheep. As we continued to walk she instructed us to pay close attention to the energy around us which was different to that on the other side of the stream. I could feel the fresh air gently blowing down through the valley which was highly relaxing. We were surrounded by trees, mainly oak trees, and I slowed down. Soaking in the atmosphere when my eyes were drawn to the stream.There, in the corner of the boulders, something caught my eye – It was the back of a sheep tucked between two rocks on the far side of the brook. Lying with her back feet in the muddy water and her head inside a hole, she was not moving but then, we noticed that she was still breathing. I rushed across to the other side of the stream and tried to lift her onto the river bank. I checked to see if she had broken a leg, but she appeared to be just dazed. I managed to lift her onto the higher ground, but as I gazed into her gentle eyes I could see she was going to give up on living. We transported her back along the path in a wheel/barrow and back at the mill we cleared her up and laid her down on the lawn. I was very upset to see this creature such a state. We attempted to give some healing to her but she was not responding. I believed she had decided to die, so we left her to rest while keeping a close eye on her.

In the meantime our teacher was going to call a farmer or somebody that could take the sheep and look after her. After ten minutes or so, a young lad came and offered to get rid of her for us if we wanted, but I told him to leave her where she was if there was going to be a problem with keeping this poor animal, I was willing to take her home with us and I knew my partner would be in agreement with me on this. After eating lunch and looking after the sheep, we decided to go upstairs to finish our session, but I could not stop thinking about this poor animal.

"I am the Light that is over all things. I am the all: from me all has come forth, and to me all has reached, split a piece of wood, I am there. Lift up a stone, you will find me there."
Saying 77 – Nag Hammadi Scriptures Gospel of Thomas by Marvin Meyer
(2007).

I could not remove the image of that poor animal with its head stuck between the rocks in that freezing stream. It was breaking my heart; how could she give up on her life like that? I started to think how this little animal must have been thinking. She was lost, alone and in the middle of the woodland where there was no grass for her, frightened by this new hostile environment and overcome with exhaustion, she was giving up on life. From time to time I was observing her from the window when I noticed she was starting to move again. She was not able to stand up on four feet, but she was walking on her knees and starting to eat the grass from the lawn, so I had hope she would be fine. Thus, in a happier frame of mind, we decided to practice giving some healing, and this time it was my turn to be the patient.

I was feeling physically very good, as I laid on the massage bed, so that the others could scan my body for any signs of blockages. To their surprise they noticed that all my chakras were blocked. They were amazed that all my chakras were shutting down – only my base was open – and our teacher could not understand the reason for this. Normally you find one, two or even three chakras blocked, but it is very rare you have them all blocked!

They told me all of my chakras were shutting down yet I was feeling very healthy and at first I did not comprehend the meaning of what they were picking up - I was linking and connecting to that poor animal because I was worried about her and, even during the healing they were performing on me, I couldn't switch my mind off of the dying sheep. I was reflecting her physical status and I felt the healing was being given through my body to the poor sheep.

After the treatment we went look for the sheep, and we found her eating hungrily and regaining use of her back legs, although she was not yet strong enough to stand up on her front legs. For me, that was a miracle! When we finished, our host insisted she was going to look after the poor animal. The next morning we emailed the healer and ask how the sheep was getting on. Inside me I felt a sense of guilt about leaving that poor animal there. I was feeling emotionally very strong! But that afternoon I learnt that the sheep had died. I felt very upset and sorry because I firmly believed she had renewed hope again.

That night I chose to sleep alone in the cottage. It proved to be a very interesting night for me. This time, before going to bed, I called the Munay Ki archetypes and the archangels of the four directions to protect my space. I could feel and see during the night there were very heavy and dense energies swirling around yet I felt very safe and for the first time I slept there with no problem.

During this period I was very emotional and compassionate but at the same time I was completely detached from any of life's dramas and arguments. I was very cold and calm.

Chapter 5

Early Visions and Revelations

At this point I was starting to call in the Munay Ki Archetypes and the Archangels more often. I began really to believe in them and, most of all, trust them. Everytime I called on them, they came. Their energies surrounded me and I felt their presence surging through my hands.

One night I felt confronted by something but there was no fear within me. I called my archetypes to help me and protect my space. I was asleep and roused me I felt a presence hit me in the side of my right hip and I perceived that something was on me – I was being approached from both inside and outside. I asked for protection and the dissipation of any negativity energies around and in me, and instantly saw a massive energy moving in the room accompanied by a swirl of spiritual activities. I saw a white light and it started to channel and ground it via my feet. My left elbow felt numb and I started having difficulty to ground the energy effectively, as it seemed something was preventing this white light energy passing through my head. In fact I had the sensation that only a small proportion was making it to my feet. I started to see bigger and different movements; the mark of the jaguar (which was the Archetype I was calling in) and some reddish eyes. I immediately felt more strong, confident and safe, so I began to question who this was. 'Reveal yourself to me!' I commanded the being, repeating my order several times. Initially it appeared as an evolving shape, then a big eye with green colours and definite romboide shape. I was still demanding to reveal itself because I could not see properly who or what it was. I began to see a skull coming out from my face, but it was still not possible to identify, so I asked again and again when suddenly things came into focus and in front my eyes I was confronted by a large cobra, mouth open showing its fangs to me once I had had a clear view of it, it abruptly returned to from whence it came.

My incredible visions continued unabated night after night. In one I again noticed the presence of very heavy energies around me, making me uneasy and disturbed. I called on the Archetypes and Earthkeepers together with the four of the Archangels: Michael, Uriel, Gabriel and Raphael. I sensed much frenzied activity; turbulence in the air and flashing lights. I was not really sure what was happening but after a good ten minutes things started to settle down, and the room again took on a more relaxed atmosphere. During all of these events I felt safe whenever I called on my Archetypes and the Archangels, but still I was a bit restless and I couldn't sleep. However, once everything was more calm and relaxed, I began asking questions to the Archangels to show me where it all began, why all this happening to me, if there was any plan for me or was there anything in particular that I needed to do?

I lost track of space and time and found myself out in space and looking at all the stars. A new galaxy formed with bright bluish colours. I drifted into them and I saw what appeared to be a multi-cells organism, followed by a mix of colours of differing in brightnesses and intensities; greens, pinks and orange and beings travelling around this galaxy, a strange, translucent emerald green aura, very shiny and bright, looked busy in his spaceship, organising things while watching what seemed to be another bigger, golden aura in a master control room. A spaceship was travelling through space passing more planets and I was flying through big bare canyons, visiting new forms of beings and planets... there were planets with bright purple skies and a planet with only one single living creature – a massive octopus enveloping the barren planet with its huge tentacles. I started to understand the purpose of the spaceship - It's role was to collect organisms, cells or living creatures from all around the universe.

I dared not believe what was happening. Was I dreaming? Something was

"Know what is in front your face, and what is hidden from you will be disclosed to you, for there is nothing hidden that will not be apparent, and nothing buried that will not be raised!"
Saying 5 – Nag Hammadi Scriptures – Gospel of Thomas 2007 by Marvel Meyer

"A man's enemies will be the members of his own household".
Book Three chapter 113:295 Pistis Sophia A Coptic text Of Gnosis with Commentary By JJ and Desiree Hurtak (2003).

telling me I was only just beginning to scratch the surface and see the possibilities and realities beyond our world. I started to be more open-minded, letting the incomprehensible come to me without trying to stop it or to rationalise it with my limited mind; let the infinite to reveal itself!

The next morning we travelled to South Africa. I was very curious, to go in a place such as here to see what else I could pick up in a totally different environment, staying at a camp near the Kruger National Park. I have been to eastern Africa several times and am aware of the beauty and the biodiversity of all nature there as well as the energies that this continent has to offer. This time, more than any other, I started to view these creatures with a different eye. It now made more sense to me how these creatures and their odd forms appeared on plant Earth! They are completely unrelated to each other, but still live in perfect harmony among themselves. These thoughts were occurring to me while I was looking at a couple of giraffes, zebras, some elephants and, later on, rhinos feeding and roaming free and they fitted completely with my recent vision.

Whilst in South Africa I did not feel or experience a lot in either the visionary or energy sense. Although I continued feeding my chakras every night, I felt detached from the place. The main things I noticed were that things were grounded and had a strong sense of instinct rather than being strongly spiritual in nature.

After we landed and were in the car driving towards home, I started to again feel that pressure on my forehead. By now I knew this was my third eye opening up being accompanied by a renewed sensation of a strong spiritual connection. About two months had passed since the incredible nights I have described and during this time I had consistently fed some of my rites every night. Now I chose to extend the practice to include all my rites together, taking me about 40 minutes in total. After the ten days spent in South Africa I had been feeling a little bit depleted, but now I was definitely regaining my strength. While feeding my rites, whenever I had any small discomfort or pain, I could heal myself.

I felt the need of some guidance or assistance, maybe from somebody with similar experiences to mine. I was trying to make some sense of all these

"O, great master, let me be a teacher af men, leading them onward and upward until
they, too, are lights among men;
freed from the veil of the night
that surrounds them,
flaming with light
that shall shine among men"
Tablet II, page 11, The Emerald Tablet By Doreal

events, so I contacted the Munay Ki founders amongst others. I even participated in a workshop in London with Professor Alberto Villoldo, but despite the fact that he gave me some very positive impressions, I did not receive satisfactory answers from any of them, or what I was really seeking. I had to keep searching as I had begun to understand that my path was going to change and evolve. My inner guidance told me that Reiki and Munay Ki were not the ways; that these are only a starting point and it was best for me to go further with my research.

I needed to know more because I was being subjected to more and more strong and intense and my lack of comprehension was frustrating me. I was desperate to understand their hidden meanings and I needed to establish a link with the ones out there who were trying to tell me something.

I started to use the medicine cards and dowse to get my daily guidance, I was going to keep looking and considering my options and answers with an open mind, allowing me to progress further into my journey.

Most of the time I received my answers by either self realisation, by a particular card from *Medicine Card by Jamie Sams & David Carson,* or by other signs or coincidences. All of these methods made me reflect and reconsider things from a different perspective - slowly I was making progress! I was guided by my invisible friends to follow my inner self which made me strengthen my will. The only thing I truly knew was that I had been blessed by some gifts and I was determined to find out more. I needed to have faith and trust my source. My life was taking a different path, a path I even didn't know existed and one I didn't know the route or destination of. It was a beautiful discovery unfolding on a daily basis and the intriguing thing was I never knew what was coming next. All this was happening while I was still working and trying to lead a normal daily life. Although, the spiritual realm permeated my mind for most of my day. I realised I needed to nurture it and make it the basis of my daily life.

Strange things were still happening at the cottage. One night I went to bed with the sacred space open in the bedroom and during the night I again saw the tumultuous and disturbing energies which were moving across the room in a uniform direction together with a flashing of lights - definitely there was some battle going on. The atmosphere in the bedroom was tense but I felt safe even though I was in the middle of these stormy energies. When I felt threatened I was sending love to them and having visions at the same time. On the other hand, my partner was feeling very uneasy and restless. We made a mistake to close the sacred place for some reasons, and soon afterwards things appeared to calm down. I fell asleep and both of us had dreams of a disturbing nature. The purpose of these dreams was to create fear, and they were using what they could find inside our mind in order to influence our emotional status. And I believe, often we get manipulated without knowing it. dreamed that the phone was ringing it was the middle of the night and it was my sister wanting to speak with me. It was nothing important and I was very annoyed with her, because she woke me up. Then my partner stood up and threatened to sleep elsewhere. At first I could not care less, but then I started to be worried for both her and myself, that we needed to stay together. On realizing it was all merely a dream, I tried to wake up but I was not able to move. It was as though something was inside me and trying to take over my body. I fought to regain my sense and mobility and eventually, after ten or twenty seconds, I managed to free myself form it, and I saw something flying out and over me.

It was time to return to the Munay Ki teacher to receive the last two rites – those of the Starkeepers and Creator. Another beautiful experience with full of colours and strong vision and one thankfully without tragedy this time. What I remember from these rites was that, during the practice of a healing session, we were supposed to heal by concentrating on a particular problem or issue. I could not think of any issue or problem I had to work on I thought very hard about what I needed to concentrate on but there was nothing I could think of that was a problem for me, so I made one up to make my healer happy. However during this session something triggered an energy to rush up and down from my heart to my left shoulder. I could feel the energy running from one end to the other, giving the sensation of hot liquid running though my nervous system, and I was being told it could be an old wound – crystallised energies being dissolved into liquid. When the healing was finished I felt an aching pain throughout my left arm and chest. Everybody was convinced that whatever it was had been dissipated during the healing session, but I still could feel it in the days to come almost as if there was a hole in my chest. I fed my rites and found when I was concentrating on my heart chakra, my hands stayed there for very long time. I was trying to heal myself!

Chapter 6

Proving Myself

I was feeding my rites every night and I was becoming very sensitive to detecting the energies of my chakras. The energies travelled within my body and even through my teeth. The first few times these energies left me out of breath, and made me sweat.

One Sunday afternoon at the cottage, I was relaxing by reading in the living room. I could see the last rays of the day with the sunset making the room very warm and bright. While enjoying the moment, I started to have some thoughts about the intrusive spirits influencing this cottage, giving me sleepiness nights and trying to scare me. These thoughts were persistent and very clear and they were guiding me to their source. Late in the afternoon it was revealed to me that source lay situated about 300 metres southwest of the cottage. I was surprised and stunned by this. There were only a couple of green bushy trees in the middle of a bare harvested field. Located in these bushy trees, I was being told, I will find some ancient stones. I had seen these trees many times, while I was out walking with my dogs, but never paid any attention to them. But now, looked at them differently. There was nothing around them. They were located a little off centre in the gently sloping field and I sensed the energies were coming from there. I started to ask more questions: Why come to this cottage if they could go to other places? The answer was that they could come into this cottage only because there were stones below the cottage which linked the house to the middle of the field. The cottage link was located in the downstairs bedroom where I was sleeping. I went to look in the bedroom, and as I started to pace the floor I noticed that something was moving below the carpet. On raising the carpet I noticed there was a crack in the concrete. raising my curiosity and making me eager to find out more. I called my partner and told her about my discovery, and how it had been revealed to me. It all made perfect sense to me now and I asked her to come over, so I could show her my findings.

I decided to leave the cottage for the night as I sensed it was not safe for me to stay there and slept soundly until something woke me up at around 3am. hovering resembled an orb very close to me and the connected to me! I started to feel energies flowing into me, rushing through my body. I saw an alien as the light was moving down to my solar plexus area but remained calm as it didn't feel negative, heavy or oppressive. These energies gave me a sense of re-assurance and love once they reached the solar plexus, making my stomach become like a fire; indeed all of my lower torso was burning hotly. I realised by then that I was starting to channel and ground an enormous amount of energy and the strangest part of this visitation was that my upper body felt entirely normal, whereas the lower part was flowing past and freely very fast with wildly hot energies.

In the morning I felt full of energy and also had acquired a strong sense of duty to go into the field where the portal was located and close it down. This urge was unstoppable.

Later that same morning the instructions as to how to close this place came. I wrote them down and saw how and what to say to seal the place. It consisted of an affirmation and prayer, together with the placing of a symbolic cross with clear intent on each of the cardinal directions around the stones. I felt no fear - I was determined to close the portal. Bearing in mind that for me this was all new, I was determined to do what I felt was right. On returning from work I fed my rites and it was about four-thirty, I was ready to go.

Earlier in the day I told my partner of my intention and she agreed to go with me but now was not willing. I was sure of what I needed to do, with or without her, so even if she tried to stop me I was determined to proceed with my plan. I wanted, to take a couple dogs with us, while performing this ceremony to close this portal as I thought taking the dogs with me would avoid any unwanted attention from the farmer. As my partner didn't want join me, I told her to take the dogs into an adjacent field instead.

Before approaching my target I was trying to ground myself, connect with my guides and request their help. That winter's afternoon was the strangest afternoon of all. I considered the air was very tense, the sky was very dark and cloudy and the biting wind was bitterly cold, so cold it was hurting my hands. Once I had reached the trees I discovered there was a small spring of water flowing over some stones. I had never been to this spot before, but my thoughts regarding the place were right. I could not see exactly where the water was coming from because of the vegetation, but I was positive this was the right spot.

At this point I felt very strong physically but I was finding it hard to concentrate. I had difficulty even to speak. Buffeted by the strong wind, I was struggling to remember the crucial words. I took a small compass from my one pocket which I thought to bring to set the cardinal directions and then from my other pocket I took my piece of paper and started to read. Once I had commenced my ritual I found it easy to carry on, even though I was still finding it difficult to mouth the words. I was confused but I did not need to think, I needed merely to read what I had written with such strong intent. Then I saw that one of my dogs had escaped and had come to see where I was. I tried to chase him away but it was futile and I was very worried for him and the distraction he was causing me that could take me away from my task. I was getting sidetracked; I needed to carry on with what I was doing and ignore him until the end of my ceremony to close this portal of energies. I went around the stone twice to make sure I did it right, and then I went around the stones three more times, imagining a cross of fire on each direction and a circle of Light around the place to seal it completely, and to connect all the cardinal directions together. Just as I was going around for the last time I heard my partner shouting in the distance, but I could not understand anything because the wind was very strong. She came towards me with the other dogs, one of whom had her head coated in blood, from a deep wound in her ear.

Despite all the diversions I believed I had managed to accomplish what I had set out to do, so I headed back up to the cottage. On noticing that another of my dogs was limping on his back leg I knew that these spirits had really tried to stop me!

Back at the cottage my partner immediately took the cut dog to the vet while I stayed, determined to finish my mission. I took my piece of paper, and I read the affirmations in the bedroom to close the links from all the directions. My hands were burning with the energies. Once I had finished I looked outside the bedroom window and saw a large flock of crows passing very close, all moving eastward with the black clouds carried by the strong wind - such surreal imagery. Then, in a matter of a few minutes, the wind suddenly eased, and everything became peaceful again. I saw the young farmer on his quad bike encircle the trees where I had been an half an hour earlier and concluded that there far were too many coincidences! At that moment I sensed, I had really closed the place or portal where the negatives energies or spirits were coming from.

I felt that these spirits could influences people's behaviour and make us do things that we normally would not do. Based on this experience, I understood how easy it is to empower them. It is only through fear and hate that they will have control of us and it is only our fear which make them strong! It is our fear that enables them to attach themselves into and prey on us.

I felt exhausted when I went to bed but I still woke up in the middle of the night, aware of lots of energies around me. I woke my partner and asked her if she could see anything. Still half asleep she told me it was nothing to worry about, reassuring me that it was merely a friendly little alien, before she went swiftly back to sleep.I tried to see them and was asking questions but I did not manage to get much out of them although in moment I felt they were trying to show me things and, while I was focusing on that thought my partner turned in her sleep and said, 'You can go with them – its safe!' Before going to sleep again. Beyond that point do not remember anything else that happened that night and, when I asked my partner in the morning about this episode, she did not have a clue what I was talking about.

It was eight months later, when I was reading a book by Dr Norma Milanovich – '*We, The Arthurians*' – that I saw a drawing of these beings, produced by one of the author's colleagues following the Arthurians' guidance about their physical appearance, and I recognised them straight way, they were the same aliens I saw in the early days and again more recently! It's true when they say they would not win a beauty contest on our planet Earth!

These were the last notable events at the cottage and I no longer picked up any heavy or dense energies. Soon it was time for me to move out and move on.

Chapter 7

Journies to the Underworld – Retrieval of my Contract

I was meditating every day and feeding my rites. During these times, I started to see with my inner eye. This brought lots of odd visions which I couldn't make any sense of, more and more I had urge to speak with somebody experienced who would know what all this means. In order for me to understand if I was following and doing the right things, did I need to do more? Did I need to stop? I began praying to God, asking if He could show me the way to go and what to do. I knew for sure that none of this was my imagination and I was determined to find the reasons for it. As I couldn't find any satisfactory answers or explanations from anyone else, I went along with my meditations. Every time called the directions and my guides I could feel their real presence with me. Many energies were running through my hands and I was getting more and more attuned to these energies. The more I fed my chakras and rites, the more was I felt my energy field, my aura. Initially, it was hard to feed my chakras/rites for more than an hour every day, but gradually it got easier and I was able to stay longer and longer performing my rituals.

Sometime I had difficulty to attune and relax because of the noise and distractions around me. I was amazed how sensitive I was becoming to hearing everything, but I was stubborn enough to carry on – and the more I carried on, the easier it became. My medicine cards and dowsing were my ways to get some answers but to progress further I kept mind open like small child, considering everything is possible and ignoring the adult rationality or common sense sent to sabotage my path. I developed a strong desire to learn as much as possible and to this end I read many more books, devouring them one after the other. One interesting book I was reading at that time was called '*Mending The Past And Healing The Future With Soul Retrieval*' by A. Villoldo. sparked my curiosity about how to retrieve and heal the soul using a South American Shamanic traditions.

Again, I had no clue what it entailed when I started to read, but in it I found some very intriguing meditations based on visualization. I would seriously recommend anyone reading this book and attempt the meditations with discretion, respect and, if possible with the help of somebody experienced and attuned to the spiritual realm. I was amazed, how through visualizations, one can tap into the unknown in different dimensions.

I started to learn new techniques and ways to meditate; how to visualise and journey, and while I was reading about them, I was trying them myself.

One Sunday night I was on my own though it was late I was so awake, I thought I would try the meditation described in the book I had read that day. My first meditation was to journey to the Lower World, and enter the first chamber; The Chamber of Wounds. The aim was to reach my soul and try to find my original wounds, healing them and therefore reassuring my soul by confronting my past, only then could I go and visit the other chambers, allowing me to re-program myself for the future. I didn't know what to expect, but I felt ready for it. I re-read the instructions carefully and tried to memorise them. I started relaxing and opening my directions and sacred space. Calling my guides, I started to visualise this journey. It amazed me how easy it was for me to visualise and move my consciousness beyond the present reality. I was trying to follow the instruction by calling one of my guides to be with me on this journey. I felt the connection on my third eye was getting stronger and stronger. The first name that came into my mind was Jesus, so I called Him.

Immediately I could feel a lovely presence around me, followed by a Light, which I associated with Him. Together, we entered in a wonderful place near to a river, I remember it was so serene and tranquil, full of colourful trees and flowers. Approaching the riverbank we called the Gatekeeper. I recognised the Gatekeeper as Caront from 'The Divine Comedy' by Dante, with his little wooden boat crossing the river. The book stresses the need to ask permission to enter the Underworld before embarking on the boat, and if the permission is denied by the Gatekeeper, do not insist, just leave and perhaps try in a later meditation. However my permission to enter was granted.

The river was calm. On reaching the other side of the river it was dark and I started to see many evil spirits surrounding and staring at me, this was unexpected so I turned to Jesus but He told me not to worry; just trust and follow Him.

In that place I saw many grotesque spirits, but one particularly frightening figure made my hair stand up and my aura vibrate. Glancing over my shoulder I saw a vile face glaring at me. I believe it was the image of death. Although one side of his face was in shadow it was a burnt asher white in colour. It chilled me to the bone for several seconds!

With all these evil spirits around me I was treading very carefully, although remembering the words of Jesus, I felt protected. I could not stop to think, I must go back the way I came in! Jesus told me to stay close, we walked through a tunnel, bringing us out into a cave with a golden light emanating from it. Jesus told me that from there I needed to go on my own.

I obeyed His command. and pressed on into the cave alone. Inside there was a woman wearing golden armour. Standing next to a Well made of stones. It seemed she was waiting for me! I asked a question, but she only told me to stay still and that she had a gift for me if I would agree to receive it. I eagerly agreed and she gave me a ball of light from her hands. My physical body and aura started to shake uncontrollably, so strong was the influence of the gift, and I understood what I was seeing and experiencing, it was real! Lost track of the time but my entire body was on fire and I was aware of being lifted by an unknown power. I could feel my aura expanding infinitely and knew something was being added to my very essence. I felt full of joy, it was totally elating!

Abruptly everything stopped, and I was dragged out from the cave, hurtling backward. I was rewound back onto the boat, on to the other shore and into myself in a matter of seconds. Regaining my senses and becoming fully concious of my physical body, in that same split second my partner opened the bedroom door asking if she could enter room!

The following day, while trying to make sense of my experiences I come to the conclusion it was a good idea to return. During this meditation was I not supposed to meet my soul and ask questions, get reassurances? But nothing had happened, as it was in the book! I vowed to prepare myself better and began my work. In just two days, I re-read the book hoping to find my answers there, but I didn't. Indeed it confused me more, because in the book the meditative directions were to travel to The Chamber of Wounds, then to the Chamber of Soul Contracts, before reaching The Chamber of Grace, and moving lastly to The Chamber of Treasures, before going to the Upper World. But from my experience on that Sunday night, the book suggested to me that I had gone straight to The Chamber of Treasures!?

I needed to know more. I couldn't wait.

So, at around ten o'clock one evening I started to call the Archangel and Archetypes from each direction and with music of high vibration. I started to relax by doing the seven breath respiration, and then imagining myself with my roots going down into earth and going into an underwater river, which took me to the Garden of Heaven, and suddenly everything was exactly as it had been on my first visit. Again I called Jesus, and once again He was with me. We called the Gatekeeper and asked permission to enter, which was again granted. Then something odd happened. I believe I gave a coin to the Gatekeeper, before we boarded the boat and crossed the river. I told Jesus I had a lots of questions to ask and He told me to ask to the lady of the Well the one I met last time. Jesus told me that she would have some answers for me.

This time I had prepared my questions – What were my wounds? How had they happened? What was being given to me? This time as I saw all the demons the scare was more settled, less tense. They were still there but they did not bother me so much this time and they did not come so close. I went

"One who seek will find! For one who knocks it will be opened". Nag Saying 94 –
Hammadi Scriptures Gospel of Thomas by Marvin Meyer (2007).

across the cavern and I asked this time to be shown how to play the vision (following the book's instructions) in a way I would find easy to understand. After a few seconds it started. This time there were several figures around, but what grabbed my attention was a little boy who took my hand and led me to a little pool of water, in which I could see the reflection of an old American Indian. Then he become more playful and so I asked him if he wanted to show me anything else. He took me back to the same water pool and I started to see other images and among all these images, I saw an angel dropping somebody from the sky naked and was told that he had not obeyed (interestingly this was not the last time I had this vision)!

I knew I did not have much time left in the underworld, so I was guided to the golden cavern, where I found the lady with the armour waiting for me next to the Well of stone. I asked my questions:

'What was given to me the night before? and why?'
She answered it was a gift from God an atonement which will give me extra power and will grow with me.

I asked Why? and what is my mission?
She replied that I needed to Bring into the Light!

I did not have time to delve deeper as something was urging me to leave. I called Jesus and there He was, ready for me. I started to walk with Him I noticed his face and body start to change, and realised I was being deceived. This was not Jesus! As I recognised the imposter so, the real Jesus came along and sent him away.

As we retraced our steps, all the demons at the entrance started to attack and jump on me and Jesus was protecting me but there were too many of them, in that moment I felt lost, confused, shocked and clueless as to what to do. There were overcome me; and I was started to panic trying to thrust them away. Suddenly I thought to expand my aura and expand the light within me a tactic which worked for some, but I still had some attached to me. I reached the riverbank and told the Gatekeeper to make sure that none of them left this world or followed me. He replied that was indeed his job, and I saw him turning and making a slow wide movement forward with his open arms as he pushed all the spirits back again, but they were so angry at me, they kept coming all the time. So Jesus told me to get into the boat quickly. I was worried that some of them were still following us and infact, when I reached the other side of the river I saw a couple that had indeed managed to cross over. I tried to push them away, but stood no chance; they were still trying to attach themselves onto me. Instead of attempting to push them back I told them they were also creatures of God, but their world was not this one and when the time was right they will be judged according to their sins. I gave them love. Understanding their situation, I felt compassionate towards them, and I saw one of them being transformed into a flower, and another into a tree near the river.

So I managed to leave the place. Although I was shocked by this visit, I was determined to return at some future time. I needed to get to the bottom of all this, if I wanted to proceed further. The message was now clear to me: "I need to Bring to the Light." But what did that mean?

That night the bedroom was not peaceful. My partner was restless and I could sense that there was heavy energy around us. I could see and feel it too. Again there was fighting going on. So I called the spirit of the Jaguar Otorongo and Archangel Michael to clear the room and afford us some protection. Then I saw a mass of white energy swivel around above me, and I felt guilty because I knew that I was the reason for the presence of these negative energies that was troubling my partner.

I thought maybe I should go back into the Underworld to the Chamber of Wounds and try to understand what was going on. Maybe I had left something unfinished? So I attempted to return again. I called the Gatekeeper and asked permission to cross the river, but to my surprise my request was denied. He told me it was not possible for me to go into the chamber.
As instructed I did not insist but came back with thoughts that I need to try again. Before I closed my eyes to sleep, I opened my safe space, and this time I slept very well.

In the morning I told my partner what had happened during the night and on my journeys into the Underworld and she was very worried.

After my experience in the Underworld I could see and feel energies around me, but I could not be sure if they were good or bad. Sometimes I could feel cold energies around my neck, and from the corner of my eye I could see the movement of energies around me. I was aware of other presences and I would often call the Jaguar and Archangel Michael to protect me. When they were with me I felt secure.

At this time my connection with my third eye was very strong and within me, I knew I was following the Will of God, through my meditations, studies, and self-realization. I was increasing my vibration, state of consciousness, awareness within myself and of everything around me. However I still needed to return and finish my mission in the Underworld.

When that time was right I opened my sacred place, and I descended to the Underworld once more, following the same meditation with the intention of understanding the happenings during my previous visits.

Once there, I called Jesus and together we called the Gatekeeper. When I asked permission to cross over, he surprised me by taking some time to respond to my request, finally granting it.

This time when I reached the other side I saw all the spirits were there lined up waiting for me. I went to them and stated my intention of coming in peace and I proceeded towards the cave. Once inside I entered a room and saw high mountains and skies with many rapidly changing images. It was very difficult for me to concentrate on what I was seeing before being led into a further new room, resembling the interior of a castle with walls constructed of large stones. Here, I found myself facing a vividly bright ray of light. I vaguely remember asking questions and clearly the answer "Bring to the Light" was voiced! The vision of the angel dropping the naked man was repeated and again I was told he had disobeyed. After a year of searching I finally understood - it was the fall of Adam from the heavens!

"When Eve was in Adam, there was no death. When she was separated from him, death came. If she enters into him again and embraces her, death will cease to be. Page. 174, Nag Hammadi Scriptures Gospel of Philip by Marvin Meyer (2007).

"So God created man in his own image, in the image of God he created him; male and female he created them. Genesis 1:27 Holy

"Within the Fall of Adam there are seven level of truths and it is the beginning for the end"

They said to him "Tell us how our end will be." He answered, "Have you discovered the beginning, then so that you are seeking the end? For where the beginning is the end will be. Blessings on one who stands at the beginning: that one will know the end and will not taste death!"

"Adam came from great power and great wealth but he was not worthy of you. For had been worthy, he would not have tasted death."
Saying 18 and 85 – Nag Hammadi Scriptures Gospel of Thomas by Marvin Meyer (2007).

It was now time to turn around and confront all the demons and spirits that before were attacking me. I found myself in a dark room with a low ceiling where they started to surround me. I reiterated that I had came in peace. Despite my limited knowledge and understanding I was willing to find out the purpose of my visit which I did not comprehend but I believed God sent me here for a reason–maybe to shed His Light among you, which I would do without hesitation. I said, for the ones willing to learn their lessons, and show their good intentions, they would see the Light again but for those who show bad intentions, the Light would be denied and they would live in the darkness for ever! I finished my discourse by ordering them not to follow me heading back to the boat and to the present realm.

Afterwards I felt so good, I knew I had accomplished one big part of my mission. I remembered the phrase *"Bring into the Light"* was of vital importance but I had no idea why!

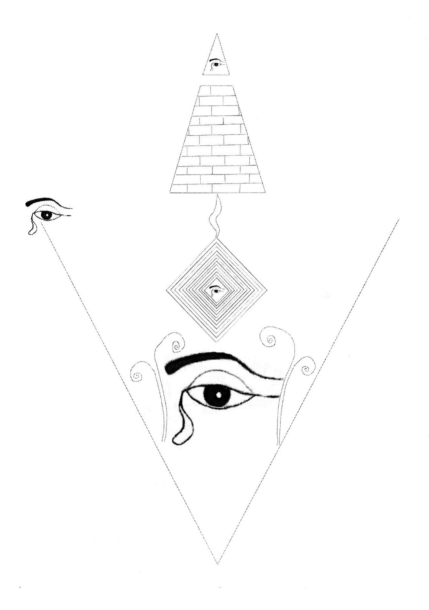

Chapter 8

My Covenant Renewed

I felt healthy, my energy was very dense. I could visualise my energy field and make it expand, and fill the room easily. When I was feeding my rites, my hands seemed as if they were sinking into my body, especially on my Third Eye, there were dense liquid energies surrounding me and I realised that I could manifest good as well as bad energy. I had to make a choice and accept the responsibility that comes with it. The easiest path would be to bow to the ego's desires, and feed it the negativity it craves.

In the following weeks I began to unveil how humanity has evolved, recognising the role of our ego in the evolution of humanity and why some secrets have been deliberately kept from all of us, maybe for our own good.

Man has known about the presence of spirits and how to connect with them, since his early time on Earth, and he has also known how spirits can apply their will by influencing the will of mankind. The ancient civilizations knew how to connect with the spirit worlds - they understood that we are their emanation. We do depend on them but also, more importantly, they depend on us too. We are their leaven! Many thoughts were coming to me about ancient people - their rituals and ceremonies, their wars, how they constructed their cities and temples using their acquired knowledge so that they could connect and indwell with their spirits. It was also at this time that I started to acknowledge the presence of Gatekeepers in churches or other sacred places as they are the protectors of sites. We must always be respectful within these places and acknowledge their presence, requesting their permission to enter.

Man on his own is a destructive force he is manipulated by spirits both from within and without. Fallen spirits rely on closing the mind of humanity using time and space boundaries to create a forgetting status, and trying to draw negative thought forms deep into our conciousness, causing our vibrations to stay low. They can control us, surprisingly easily and make us believe in a finite reality limiting and enslaving us to our five senses, co-creating fear and poverty within and without us and, in doing so, causing us to destroy both our surroundings and ultimately, ourselves.

"The Lord of Light warned man not to misuse the Language of Light, by using the wrong ebb and flow of the language patterns, or by using the knowledge of the language against the Will of the Father. But man did not hearken to the Word of the Lord and accepted instructions from fallen Ophanim under the command of Semjaza, who shared many of the Eternal secrets of the Father's Kingdom which men were striving to learn. However, these secrets were shared through the art of warfare, the art of spoken and written language which was corrupted and segmented, resulting in imperfect scriptures, and other arts enchanting man and leading him astray.
The fallen instructors also taught the arts of temple building and architecture, and instructed man to build great cities with towers for communication that would unify man with the hierarchy of the fallen angels. Michael, Uriel, Raphael and Grabriel looked down from heaven and saw how the lawlessness on the planet was being used by the fallen angels to extend their knowledge to other planetary kingdom. They appealed to the Throne of YHWH to put an end to the Tower of Babel and blind the eyes of fallen humanity from the language of Light."
Hurtak, The Book of Knowledge, Keys of Enoch. Keys 214:39-43

I was progressing well with my studies and meditation but there was still a degree of tension in my private life, I was trying my best to keep it away from me and I noticed that I wasn't holding any resentment or anger, I believed more than ever that all of my past bad feelings had now gone. I felt clear-minded and lighter; the proud attitude and defensive behaviour was no longer part of me. I wasn't feeling hurt any more and nursed no resentment. I felt great!

Often, when an argument occurs, it is past emotions feeding into a current situation. By doing that, we are giving our Light away. We are <u>decreasing</u> our chances to <u>increase</u> our vibration and reach the higher state of Mind. Now, the past appeared so remote to me; it could no longer touch me. I felt completely detached from everything and everyone. I understood the meaning of the native peoples of South America when they say "Sachamama: who wraps the coils of Light around us and teaches us to shed the past - as he sheds his skin!"

One night, I was in bed and I switched the light off. I felt the need to open my directions and, in the dark, I saw a lot of energies gathering around. I could not distinguish what they were but my connection through my Third Eye was strong. I therefore asked the Munay Ki Archetypes and Archangels to help me to create protection and let me see more clearly. I also called in the animal spirits, which I had found in my medicine cards book. Every time I read that book I found much wisdom in it as I learnt the characteristic and significance of each animal.

My forehead was burning hot, and this feeling must have lasted for hours. It was a beautiful sensations and, as I started to tap into other dimensions, I found myself wandering in the infinity of the universe where shapes, colour, and forms of energy prevail - where matter has not been created yet. It was a flow of energy from start to finish, with indescribable geometrical shapes, colours, colours and formations of stars that I dove into. My body was shaking and I felt full of love. I wanted to scream for joy! The sensation was so great that I could not be contain it within me and it was as if I was going to explode. At one point I heard what sounded like/broadcasting in a radio frequency very harsh accented language, but I didn't understand what was being said I was so focused on the excitement of the visual experience.

In the morning when I got up, I picked three medicine cards trying to make a sense what had happened the previous night. The answers were that I was within the Universal Mind and I need to give time to digest a comprehend the real meanings of it.

I carried on and re-read the end of the Upper World of the book *Soul*

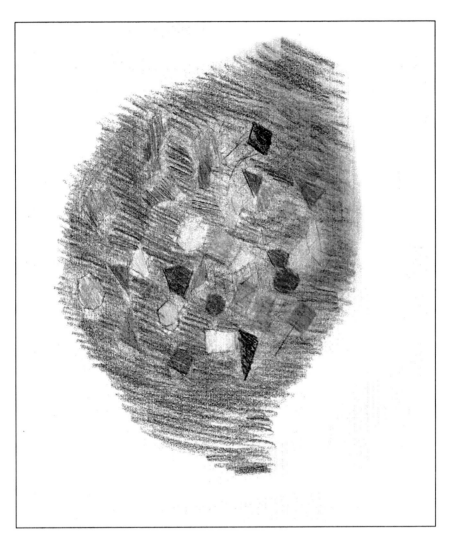

" I shall give you what no eye has not seen, what no ear has heard, what no hand has touched, what has not arisen in the human heart."
Saying 17 – Nag Hammadi Scriptures Gospel of Thomas by Marvin Meyer (2007).

Retrieval by Alberto Villoldo, where there is a very important meditation which brings one to the Upper World, then to the fifth world or dimension. Here the aim is to get in touch with the Original Self or Higher Self, and receive etheric gifts that enable us to proceed on the spiritual journey. I remember Dr. Alberto Villoldo saying that we should go to the Upper World and meet our Higher Self as often as possible. I had tried to do this meditation several times at night but, for one reason or another, I had never managed to reach the place where I needed to be. But that night, I considered it was the right time and I was determined to finish and accomplish this meditation.

So, I relaxed myself and went up through the Tree of Life and met the Gatekeeper who promptly let me in, before meeting up with my celestial parents, who according to Dr. Villoldo are the holders of our contract containing our mission on Earth. I asked to be led to see my Original Self. Eventually, I managed to find him and I recognised that we were the same, but I could see the Light of him was emanating brilliantly. According to the meditation, the Original Self is supposed to help me to clear my past lives or past debts.

I was looking forward to finding out my role in this world and lifetime. The Upper World, I believed, was the place where I could best ask the questions and see if I could receive my answers. I went up several times and attempted to retrieve the information but I was obviously not ready, it was too early!

Then through my reading I found the right visualization/meditation from the book: *The Four Insights: Wisdom, Power and Grace of the EarthKeepers* by Dr. Alberto Villoldo, enabling me to ask the vital questions to proceed! The aim of this meditation was to clear the three greatest and most influential past life experiences. The meditation consisted of going to the Upper World through the Tree of Life, then reaching the Fifth World and asking the Gatekeepers permission to let me in to meet my Celestial Parents They led me to my Original Self and after meeting with Him. I asked, if he could show me the pool where I could clear my three most influential past lives and experiences the moment when they had ended. I wanted to see and feel the life that had endured the most suffering; the one in which I had most power and I had abused it (which I had not used wisely) and, finally, the life with my greatest power - which I had used wisely.

There was something very peculiar in what I experienced, which, confused me more. I couldn't understand the meaning of these visions, and while I was having them in this meditation, my phone was ringing and ringing. Different people were trying to contact me, and the dogs were also barking loudly and trying to interrupt my meditation, but my inner guidance was telling me to carry on. I believe within these are very important mysteries and those who already have the gift of understanding <u>will</u> understand. The visions evolved as follows:

The life of the most suffering - *I felt again under the pressure of time, and I saw desert sands. Then I saw a woman wearing a black dress - it was obvious that she was alone and was suffering. I saw her on her bed, and she was going to pass away on her own, so I forgave her for all the sins she had done before and I blessed her and released her from the pain and suffering into the Light. This process made my body vibrate.*

The life I had power but I misused — *I saw a powerful ruler, dressed in his armour, a garment of war. His face was overshadowed by darkness in a constant sided flow from left to right and from right to left transfiguring his face, I could see evil transpire from his skin and he was full of anger and hatred towards all the world. When he died there were people around him but they were there because they feared him. I forgave him before passed away, blessed him and released him into the Light and again my soul and body vibrated.*

The life with the great power, which I used wisely - *I saw Jesus fighting with evil. I saw Him on the cross, minutes before He passed away and I saw the pain of Mary, unable to let Him go, and at this time, when I was releasing and letting him go into the Light, the phone was ringing and ringing, but I felt the need to carry on and I ignored the phone and all the other external distractions. I blessed this vision and released it into the Light. When I finished, my soul and body resonated and I saw an opening in the sky that was welcoming me.*

"We were therefore buried with him through baptism into death in order that, just as Christ was raised from the dead through the glory of the Father, we too may live a new life. If we have been united with Him like this in his death, we will certainly also know that our old self was crucified with him so that the body of sin might be done away with, that we should no longer be slaves of sin — because anyone who has died has been freed from sin. Now if we died with Christ, we believe that we will also live with Him. For we know that since Christ was raised from the dead, he cannot die again; death no longer has mastery over him." Romans 6:4-9 Holy Bible

After this meditation I felt so liberated and full of joy. Here was yet another mystery that I could not solve, there were more and more mysteries waiting to be uncovered and understood by me, but I could not find anybody to answer my growing number of questions! Until finally in the later stage of my journey, when it all became very clear to me.

Chapter 9

Releasing the Lost Soul

Another intriguing and educational experience I had related to the ruins of the house near the woodland, once this was home of a person who deliberately took his own life. I took my dogs for a walk everyday nearby this site and everytime I was in the vicinity of these ruins I felt a strong pressure at the back of my head - similar sensations I had whilst at the cottage. I mentioned this to my partner and thought it connected to the lost soul of this person, who had hanged himself, these incidents made me more aware of the place and everytime I was passing that ruins, I became vigilant protecting myself. On one occasion the pain on the back of my head actually stayed with me. I had already been feeling in the past few days that this soul was trying to attach himself to me without success, but this time I believe achieved his aim. I tried to talk to him and advised him to be patient, and that his time will come forth. I carried on walking with my dogs, but the pressure in my head gradually increased until it was quite painful. I was walking with my partner at that time and after the walk I felt very unbalanced. That same day while I was doing my meditation with my partner- something was just not feeling right. I noticed my partner was distressed but I did not understand why, she told me it was because of the lost soul trying to attach to her! She successfully rejected him, but now I found him again trying to re-attach onto me. Unusually I felt unbalanced and confused after I had finished my meditation. This was in total contrast to my normal feelings of clarity and strength so I sensed that something was not right.

If I knew how to help him, I would have released him to the Light and set him free, but at this stage I really didn't know how to achieve this result. I felt a heavy weight almost painful on my shoulder. I tried hard to remove it, but no avail. So I tried to meditate again, and when I was attempting to journey to the Upper World in orders to get the advice I was seeking I could see the shadow of his soul over me. I had no alternative - I had to come back again and abandon the meditation. I tried everything to ground it, to decree it; but his soul remained with me I clearly remember it was greyish in colour.

Then, with my partner's help, we managed to release into the Light. It was all about trust, faith, love and compassion, which he did not want to leave because within him there was fear and loneliness. With no confidence or self-esteem, he would not trust himself to let go. But in the end my partner managed to convince him to follow the Light. What my partner was picking up was the loneliness of a misunderstood and wounded child. She felt to call in the soul of her beloved dog who had passed away a year earlier in her arms. He was the father of our four dogs and she had been devoted to him. She believed by invoking his presence and letting him accompany the lost soul, the poor lost soul would feel confident enough to leave. And she was right - as her dog was leading the lost soul to the Light, I immediately felt a release of weight as if a heavy burden had been lifted from my shoulders. In the end it was an overwhelming and highly emotional experience. Afterwards, to be sure, I decided to re-enter in a state of meditation and the grey shadow was no longer over as around me. To my great relief he had indeed crossed over into the Light.

Chapter 10

The Fight for the Light – Torch Bearer

I journied to the Upper World daily to meet my Original Self, and I would visit other worlds and during these meditations see immense landscapes. I was visiting new places and seeing new beings, it was like I was journeying into this world, I could see, but I could not hear anything.

One day, something very peculiar happened while I was in the Upper World, while waiting for my guide to take me to new places. I had been contemplating the landscape surrounding me for quite some time expecting that something or someone would appear to guide me to other places, as was normally the case, but I seemed stuck in this flat desert landscape, nothing was happening. I nearly decided to leave and come back to my present, but suddenly, while pondering what to do the landscape started to move towards me. I started to see far in the horizon, mountains, valleys, and beyond those, higher snow capped mountains. I decided to wander around the higher mountains, which were very serene and peaceful. As I stood admiring the view of the mountains and the valley below, something caught my eye so I glanced up at the sky. To my disbelief and astonishment, I saw angels fighting each other; engaged in a raging battle! They were striking each other violently and powerfully. I realised, it was a fight between the Angels of Light and Angels of Darkness, and I had the impression that they were so immersed in their battle that they had not seen me although I was right below them in their midst. I did not really want to be noticed by them. The Angels of Light were emanating a bluish light from their golden armour, whereas the other angels were wearing dark armour, from which no light was radiating. I spotted a watch tower made of stone; circular in shape topped by a domed roof positioned on top of the highest mountain. A light shone within the tower, drawing me towards what resembled more as a Hellenic temple. Carefully, I went just under their battleground and slowly I flew up reaching the top of the mountain and entered the tower. I was exceedingly curious as to what I would discover inside. A wooden torch burnt brightly in the middle of the room! Without hesitation seized it with both hands and, once it was firmly in my grasp, it started to glow ever brighter and brighter and brighter, burning with golden white light, and then it started to expand. The light was so intense that my eyes could no longer cope with its brilliance - it was blinding me!

Through the brightness, I suddenly saw the battling angels - except now they had stopped fighting and were instead turning their attention to me, they were looking at me as I stood holding The Torch of Light, they appeared surprised. The Torch was sending rays of Light everywhere, enveloping everything including the angels in its glare. My body itself started to became a beam of white light, so bright and radiant that I could not look at it.

I had no idea, what to do, so I decided to leave and while I attempting to descent to my present earthly consciousness, my body become covered by flames and fire. As I reached the Fifth World my Celestial Parents stopped me from descending further. They told me that I needed to use love and compassion and, when I followed their advice and starting to be in a state of mind of love and compassion, my body once again returned to bright white light, not burning fire.

I left the Upper World in a state of bright white light, and once I was back my face and my body were on fire, burning without flames. Now I knew that I had seen a bigger picture of all that everything is in life and this gave me a great sense of responsibility. I understood instantly it was not just our Mother Earth at stake; but rather the entire Universe was involved in this battle.

"Perhaps people think that I have come to impose peace upon the world. They do not know that I have come to impose conflicts upon Earth, fire, swords and war. For there will be five in the house: there will be three against two and two against three, father against son and son against father, and they will stand alone."

"Show us the place where you are, for we must seek it. He said to them, whoever has ear should hear. There is a Light within a person of Light, and when it shines it shines on the whole world and if it does not shine, it is dark!"
Saying 16 and 24 – Nag Hammadi Scriptures Gospel of Thomas by Marvin Meyer (2007).

I understood that I needed to be patient and embrace humility in order to go further in my path. This last vision really left a lasting impression on me and forced me to think about many things about this illusional reality that we live here on Earth. That night I was tired but I was restless and could not sleep. I was sensing masses of energy in the bedroom and the pressure in my forehead was getting stronger. I was thinking about the American Indians – how much suffering, humiliation and pain they have endured, and how they were often forced to leave their land. Earlier in the day I started to read the book *'The Wind is my Mother, The Life and Teaching of a Native American Shaman' by* Bear Heart (with Molly Larkin), which is where I got this sense of hardship from. Later by following my inner guidance I understood how to use the energies for the greater good. I was able to call the directions, then create a ball of Light and keep it in front of me, filling it with my desires and wishes before sending it to heal the world.

I started going every morning to the top of a field from where I would perform this ritual, sending healing both to the animals that were at risk of extinction and also to the heart of man. I was doing this in my morning walks. My need to help all aspects of the natural world being decimated by the greed of man was overwhelming. So I was directing this energies to soften the hearts of these men, making them more compassionate towards our Mother Earth, and also I used to send healing to people that I knew were having very difficult times. And I did this every morning and sometimes in the night.

In these days, I was recalling the compassion and awareness that was ruling the life of the American Indians. The natives embraced oneness and instinctively knew how to unfold sacred nature; how to tap into the vastness of the infinite, that universe within all of us within each and every single living creature. They comprehended how to sustain balance and unite the state of within, together with the without, to live as one in this spiral of harmony and love!

Chapter 11

The Searching for Help

After I saw the battle of the angels, I felt more and more the need for deeper knowledge, I was trying to interpret accurately the messages from the cards that I was still picking on a daily basis, to assist me unveil the truth. A kind lady I had met while at one of the workshops I had attended asked me, it is good to have lots of energies and be gifted, but what was I going to do with them? I still didn't know what God wanted me to do! How I could serve Him here on earth. It was easer to say that I knew what I did not want to do, which was open a workshop and making a living from it. I did not see me doing this in conjuction creating a business from it and I knew my mission was different, but I did not yet realise what it was! She advised me to contact the founder of one of the well-known spiritual organizations, had great experience in the spiritual field and may be able to help shed some light on my visions and help me understand my direction. I considered this useful advice and so I wrote an email and then followed this up with a phone call, but unfortunately the answer from all these organizations is that, without paying a considerable sum of money, it is not possible to speak with the person who had been recommended to help me and assisting in the comprehension of my experiences. I remember I wrote an email describing the last two strong visions and physical sensations I'd had in the past weeks, which were those visions/experiences filled symbols and colours and the one of the fighting Angels. These visions had left an extremely strong imprint in my mind, and I was on a quest to understand their meanings. I was wondering if any of the people I contacted had undergone similar experiences to mine, but sadly I could not find any answers from these people, only further disappointment. Their main aim appeared to be to enrol me in their extremely expensive courses, or have a series of prolonged phone conversation at the rate of several hundred dollars per hour. On principle, and aide of my invisible guides, I dismissed both options. I believed that if all this was coming from the Most High, there was no way He was supporting this level of mercenary pricing to help another soul.

> *"Let someone who has found the world and has became wealthy renounce the world!"*

> *"No buyers and merchants will enter the places of my Father". Nag Saying 110 and 64:12 – Hammadi Scriptures Gospel of Thomas by Marvin Meyer (2007).*

A week later, one of the sales guys of one organization called me again trying to sell me the benefits of their courses, but after a brief conversation, I said to him: '*There are many paths but only one way.*' certainly I did not believe their way was the way! Running concurrently to this I was having a lot of dreams about these organizations, in which I was being sent messages warning me that some of these groups were using their spiritual gifts to manipulate and convince people to do their courses. I was told by my inner guidance that I could go further on my own, and for the good of all. So I decided, after much temptation, to let go and rely more on where my true spiritual guides were going to lead me. I followed what for me was the higher guidance, which told me these organizations are not the way.

I continued to seek knowledge in my own way to attempt to decipher and understand the unfolding truth. I was being told by my invisible guide to have faith and the true way to the Light is by taking the path of "Wisdom". Spiritual gifts request responsibility in order to go further and please our God. Everything needs to be measured and balanced for the good of all. This is the way to create Heaven on Earth!

I knew that my enemies were very close and that they have the power to manipulate, deceive and empower my ego more. I understood their aim: to create separation, destruction, reaction and anger, to disconnect the heart and just be self-centred.

I desperately wanted to know how? What? Where? Why? When? And I wasn't going to give up until I found my answers or achieved my goal. I wanted to know and understand now and my persistence was resulting in frustration rather than celebration.

"Two will rest on a couch; one will die, one will live,
Salome said, who are you, mister? You have climbed onto my couch and eaten from my table as if you are someone.
Jesus said to her, I am the one who comes from what is whole. I was given from the things of my Father.
I am your follower.
For this reason I say, If one is whole, one will be filled with Light, but if one is divided, one will be filled with darkness."
Saying 61 – Nag Hammadi Scriptures Gospel of Thomas by Marvin Meyer
(2007).

Part Two

In this section of the book I have been guided to write about my new state of being. I was approaching the unknown with a more peaceful state of mind than before. I was no longer the only " different" or "fortunate" one; I was one of many, one of unity of force, one of compassion, one of discernment, and embracing more the power of humility, respecting and accepting the outcome.

"It is the God within us, The Father/Mother does it all."

At this stage I had very strong visions. Physically, I started to experience downloads on a daily basis, and I also suffered strong pain on the left side of my body, affecting my shoulder and arm. But the hardness in the heart was easing off slowly, provided that I kept monitoring my thoughts and emotions!

"I must go on boasting. Although there is nothing to be gained, I will go on
to visions and revelations from the Lord."
2 Corinthians 12:1

"Even if I should choose to boast, I would not be fool, because I would be
speaking the truth. But I refrain, so no one will think more of me than is
warranted by what I do and say.
To keep me from becoming conceited because of these surpassingly great
revelations, there was given me a thorn in my flesh, a messenger of Satan, to
torment me. Three times I pleaded with the Lord to take it away from me.
But he said to me 'My grace is sufficient for you, for my power is made perfect
in weaknesses.' Therefore I will boast all the more gladly about my
weaknesses, so that Christ's power may rest on me." 2 Corinthians 12:7-9
Holy Bible

Chapter 12

The Initial Transformation – Starting the Healing Process

Few weeks after the vision of battle of the angels started to have a strong sensation of heaviness again, located mainly in the centre of my spine just behind my heart chakra. It became very uncomfortable and sometimes I felt it around and inside my body. My first thoughts were that maybe it was the lost soul of the man in the woods, but then it felt different. One time, as I was driving to work and I felt this energy moving to my right eye and causing me pain. Interestingly enough I was able to feel it with my hand so, whilst still driving, I grabbed and dislodged it, making the pain instantly disappear. However, after a few minutes, it retuned, I did this several times. Following this I spent many days and nights trying to remove this alien energy. The sensation was like a jelly fish with tentacles that left my skin irritated each time I pulled them away. This entity was definitely stopping me from expanding the light whereas before I could expand white/golden light without limits.

Feeding my rites dislodged it temporarily but it come back again after few minutes later burning hotter than before. After my meditation, I would not feel its presence return until I was getting agitated or rushing under these circumstances it would come back and cause me further discomfort, as if something was sitting on my back and chest. When I tried to go to the Upper World again I could see its shadow rather like the one of the lost soul, affecting the flow of energy and making my connection weaker. It was creating blockages, especially to my heart, which over time appeared to become like a rock, stopping the flow completely. I did not understand it but I knew it prevent me from following my path way to the Light. I knew it was consuming my energies and I started to feel weaker and weaker. The more I was trying to fight it the more stronger it was getting!

My partner was helping me and we tried all we could. I called my guides, archangels and angels, for their help. I tried performing an extraction with crystals. I continued feeding my rites, but this only seemed to stimulated it and made it stronger. I thought strengthening my energy fields would help but to no avail - all my efforts failed and I was exhausted. Eventually I had some significant dreams and messages through the cards that told me not to give up, but to remain faithful and true to the way, my path was all about choices - I could go either way. I needed to embrace all and not focus on one!

This was a time of great confusion and pain for me. After months of wonderful experiences. Until this point I had always been safe protected and in control of my abilities, but now I felt vulnerable and powerless. Had I done something wrong? Had I messed with something I should have left well alone? The lack of knowledge was making me terribly frustrated and searching for answer.

"You cannot enter the house of the strong and take it by force without tying the person's hands. Then you can loot the person's house."
Saying 35 – Nag Hammadi Scriptures Gospel of Thomas by Marvin Meyer
(2007).

At night I could feel it travelling around inside me from my back to my third eye and into my heart. It was always present and I could not ignore it, I knew exactly where it was lying within my body at any time. I wanted to remove it, and quickly!

Through my messages I finally understood this thing was a part of me - that part that need to be transmuted and this was a test for me. I needed to withstand the challenge and overcome it.

I began to be more accepting of it, even in the moments when its presence was strong. It dawned on me that my frustrations, upset, anger and attempts to reject it were giving it strength. A change of attitude was necessary so, rather than hating it and trying to remove it, I tried to be compassionate and to fight it with love; looking for something positive in it. In this way I managed to restore a little bit of fluidity to the energies in my essence. I could embark upon some soul travelling again and enjoy visions during my journeys, albeit aware that there were certain influences still trying to deceive me.

In one meditation I visualised myself journeying in the Upper World. The Gatekeeper allowed me to enter in with no problem but my connection was weak, I could not see well and could be disconnected very easily. I asked for my Celestial Parents and they came offering me a great comfort, I asked if I could meet with my Original Self, and questioned Him about the possibility of seeing my destiny and about this energy that was causing such discomfort to me.

He asked me - How would I like to see it? But really I did not understand what he meant, so we merged and started to travel to the future. First we went to a place far out in the universe; I did not have a clue where I was; it was like a fantasy world. The planet was bare full of holes and suddenly we jumped into one of the holes and I found myself on Earth, where I was shown the depletion and devastation of all the animal kingdom with human bodies littering the streets I wanted to cry so distraught! I saw some of the events responsible for this catastrophic scenario, which included the rising sea levels, due to the higher temperatures and the melted polar ice caps and a meteorite hitting Earth, making the sky a ball of fire. Disease and starvation – had caused the population to shrink drastically and the dead lay unburied. I asked why? But I knew the answers already. The destruction was inevitable, caused by an increasing number of people inhabitants created a situation where life was not sustainable- nature itself had closed down. What I saw was an awful global disaster but I was told that eventually all this destruction would bring balance again and a new beginning.

Whilst this scenario was absorbing me, I could feel the connection on my third eye was being covered up by this "jellyfish" energy - clinging to my head. I believe it was trying to influence or understand what was going on.

"Jesus said: I disclose my mysteries to those who are worthy of my mystery. Do not let your left hand know what your right hand is doing."
Saying 62 – Nag Hammadi Scriptures Gospel of Thomas by Marvin Meyer
(2007).

I felt very low on energy, so I asked to go to the creator place to be recharge. It was like a sun, full of Light. Last time I had been there my energy had expand so much that I could not contain it all inside my body. But this time the effect was much less and I left drained.

I closed the directions and drained down the energy sending healing to people in need before falling asleep.

When I got up in the morning I felt full of energy again, and I felt keener on sending healing out again, before leaving for work in the morning.

Later that day my partner suggested that I should contact my friends, the Reiki teachers - as it had been a while since I'd seen them. At first I was not sure, but then I decided to contact them.

I had considered all kinds of possibilities for this energy force that was bothering me. I perhaps it was something that had been left inside my essence from a previous life. It was well anchored into me through the middle of my heart chakra into my back. I felt it was trying to disconnect me from my source. But perhaps it was a good idea to get a second opinion, so I rang my friend Ann to try and arrange to meet up, I described the vision of the Battle of Angels and she immediately answered telling me it was the battle for my soul that is within me, for the first time I knew that I was being given the right interpretation of the vision/experience, unveiling at least some of it! And one that tied in with my partner advising me that it indicated a duality of good/bad in me. It would be my choice to make. It was at this point that Ann recommended I read: *"The Light Shall Set You Free"* by Dr Norma Milanovich and Dr Shirley D. McCune (ed.1997) and instructed me that I needed to read it seven times. This book opened a new path to me and it provided me with some of the answers. It was a new start for me!

My partner was still struggling with all of my progress and growth. I felt she was trying to convince me to stop, but I knew there was no way back for me. If she could not cope and accept my new way of living I would simply have to move on even after 10 years of living together. I knew that if I tried to stop or pretend that nothing was happening, let all these months of events pass without further investigation, to give up now would be the worst thing I could do! I needed to confront the situation and learn from it, no matter how difficult or painful it might be.

I needed direction and knowledge. Faith and strong determination to succeed were the only things I had!

One night I had a dream which was just before I went to meet up with Ann and Graham (her husband) to try and see if they could help me with my energy problem.

In the dream I with Reiki therapist and together we were looking for a healer to help me. I likened these energies to a jelly fish that was clinging on my skin, and she took me to a Jewish Rabbi who specialized in removing entities from one's body. When I was with him, he could not see anything, but I was insistent and could not comprehend how he could miss it what, in my dream was clearly there. The Rabbi asked where it came from? So I replied it was from the universe. Suddenly he started to judge me, warning me that I was pursuing evil by doing what I was doing. despite this he tried again and found whatever it was, and tried to pull it out. While he was struggling to remove it a white mouse bit my big toe, seeking my attention, so I asked to the little mouse what was going on, why was he biting my toe, and he warned me not to try to remove the evil in this manner as it would paralyse me, it can only be done by believers!

The coincidence was that only one day earlier my partner had dreamt that she should give me a mouse as a gift. In addition to all this, I had been getting strong messages that it was time to cleanse myself, to let go what doesn't serve me anymore.

"A person cannot mount two horses or bend two bows. And a servant cannot serve two masters, or that servant will honour the one and offend the other. No person drinks aged wine and immediately desires to drink new wine. New wine is not

poured into aged wineskins, or they might break, and aged wine is not poured into a
new wineskin, or it might spoil. An old patch is not sewn onto a new garment, for
there would be a tear. "
Saying 47 – Nag Hammadi Scriptures Gospel of Thomas by Marvin Meyer
(2007).

With all of this going on I came to the conclusion that I had the opportunity to choose now, and that I could go either way. It was up to me what I wanted to do and how I should use this gift that had been given to me, for the highest good. Sincerely believed I was fighting for my soul and had a 50/50 chance to win or lose the battle - it was all up to me!

I read the book that Ann recommended to me and thus finally brought me peace within myself. The night before seeing Ann & Graham, I was in bed after reading my book when beings of light came to see me. I had dreams, but I could not clearly make any sense of them, and at one time I thought I was channelling some energies from these beings of light.

I was looking forward to visiting my friends, getting a second opinion. On meeting them, I briefly went over my experiences of the last four months and, after some discussion, we decided to do a healing on me. The healing session lasted for a few hours and during it they saw the snake within me, which surprised us all. This was the snake I had seen a few months earlier and It was anchored mainly in my heart chakra. They were trying to remove it, but it could not be done and it was indeed foolish to try. By then, I knew whom my enemy was, and that the battle was mine and mine alone.

"Settle matters with your enemy as long as you journey on the way with him, so
that your enemy may not somehow turn you over to the judge, and the judge turn
you over to the attendant, and the attendant throw you into prison, for you certainly
will not come out before you have paid over the last little coin value."
Matthew 5:25-26 Holy Bible and Book Three, chapter 113:296 Pistis Sophia
A Coptic Text Of Gnosis with Commentary by J J and Desiree Hurtak (2007).

"Jesus said: The Father kingdom is like a person who had a good seed. His enemy

came at night and sowed weeds among the good seed. The person did let them pull up the weeds, but said to them. 'No, or you might go to pull up the weeds and pull up the wheat along with them. For on the day of the harvest the weeds will be conspicuous and will be pulled up and burned.'"
Saying 57 – Nag Hammadi Scriptures Gospel of Thomas by Marvin Meyer (2007).

The awakening raises our energy fields or our vibrations. Vibration is the spin created by molecules. The faster they go the more energy they produce, until they become light, which then enables the body to unfold into a multi layered body. It is like an opening of a rose, of which each petal is a layer. It has been written that we have nine bodies and it is my understanding that these nine bodies, once they are activated and work all in equilibrium with each other, represent our Tree of Life. After more than two years of study and research I understood that once all nine bodies are in harmony and balanced with each other and our Tree of Life is activated there will be others trees which will attach to our activated tree of life and this is the aim of human kind.

"And the Lord God commanded the man, 'You are free to eat from any tree in the garden; but you must not eat from the tree of the knowledge of good and evil, for when you eat of it you will surely die.' "
Genesis 2:16-17 Holy Bible.

"Jesus said, Blessing on one who came into being before coming into being.
If you become my followers and listen to my sayings, these stones will serve you.
For there are Five Trees in the Paradise for you; they do not change, summer or winter, and their leaves do not fall. Whoever knows them will not taste death".
Saying 19 – Nag Hammadi Scriptures Gospel of Thomas by Marvin Meyer (2007).

Within our essence there is a lower self which is in control of the densest form of all our essence and can be accessed through our chakras (our physical, emotional and mental bodies which, it is my understanding are the ones controlling our lives in this three-dimensional world). Only once one is awakened and starts to feel and see, is he not blind anymore, so it really all depends on how much one is seeking to unveil the truths!

"The woman said to the serpent: 'We may eat fruit from the trees in the garden, but God did say, you must not eat fruit from the tree that is in the middle of the garden and you must not touch it, or you will die.'
'You will not surely die,' – The serpent said to the woman. 'For God knows that when you eat of it your eye will be opened, and you will be like God, knowing good and evil.'
When the woman saw that the fruit of the tree was good for food and pleasing to the eye, and desirable for gaining wisdom, she took some and ate it. She also gave some to the husband, who was with her, and he ate it. Then the eyes of both of them were opened, and they realised that they were naked; so they sewed fig leaves together and made coverings for themselves." Genesis 3:2-7 Holy Bible.

That night when I was at home, I was asking questions, and the answers were coming to me. It cannot be removed, but I could transform it. How, I asked and during the night it came to me - it had to be with love – unconditional love! This triggered thoughts and visions that flowed into my mind, about when Jesus The Christ was riding a donkey after he was made King of Israel bringing words 'humble' and 'humility' to me, and making me understand I could reach the state of unconditional love through humility.

"If you bring forth what you have within you, what you have will save you. If you do not have that within you, what you do not have within you will kill you."
Saying 70 – Nag Hammadi Scriptures Gospel of Thomas by Marvin Meyer (2007).

I needed to use my heart on a daily basis which was not easy as since the Awakening, it had been hardened. I needed to talk, walk, live and feel more with it. I was thinking how many times I said please or thank you, but it was only with my head and not with my heart. So I visualised putting lips, eyes and feelings back to my heart, and once I did that, my heart began to open and ease off with a tremendous sensation of freedom and relief. It was all about using my heart and being more humble - it was that simple! The snake remind me to be humble and embrace humility to think with my heart and not with my head. The simple realisation overwhelmed me.

We virtues are in God and we remain in God,
we are soldiers for the King of Kings
and we overcome evil by good.
For we began visible in the first action
where we existed as victorious,
while that one fell to the ground who wished to fly above God.
Therefore let us even now be soldiers,
coming up to aid those who call upon us,
and trampling on the skills of the devil,
and leading through to blessed mansions
these who will have wished to imitate us.

The complaint of the souls placed in a body
Alas, we are strangers.
What have we done, straying into sins?
we ought to be daughters of the King,
but into the shadow of sins we fell.
O Living Sun,
Carry us on your shoulder
into the most righteous inheritance,
which we lost through Adam!
O King of Kings,
we are fighting in your battle.

The invocation of the Faithful Soul
O sweet Divinity
and pleasant Life,
in which I will wear a bright garment,
accepting the one which I lost in my first appearance,

to you I sigh and I invoke all the virtues.

The answer of the Virtues
O happy soul,
and o sweet creature of God,
you who have been built on the profound height of
the wisdom of God,
you love much.

The Faithful Soul
O freely I will come to you
in order that you may offer me the kiss of your heart.

Virtues
We ought to serve as soldiers with you,
o daughter of the King.

But the burdened soul complained
O the heavy labor and harsh weight
which I have in the Garment of this life,
because it is very hard for me to fight against the body.

Virtues
O soul, created by the will of God,
and o happy instrument,
why are you so weak against this body
which God created with a virgin nature?
You ought to overcome the devil with us.

The Soul
Hasten to help me,
so that I might be able to stand.

Knowledge of God speaks to the Soul:
See what it is
In which you have been clothed, o daughter of salvation,
And be firm and you will never fall.

That Soul:
Oh I do not know what I may do or where I might flee to;
Oh woe to me, for I am not able to perfect this body in
which I am clothed.
I surely wanted to cast it away.

Virtues:
O unhappy conscience,
O wretched soul,
Why do you hide your face in the presence of your Creator?

Knowledge of God to that soul:
You do not know neither do you see nor understand
The one who created you.

That Soul:
God created the world, I do not harm the world,
But I do want use it.

The suggestion of the devil speaks to the same soul:
Foolish, foolish
What do you bring forth by your work?
Serve the world,
And it will embrace you with great honor.

Virtues:
Alas, Alas
Let us virtues bewail and mourn,

Because a sheep of the Word flees life.

Humility:
I humility,
Queen of the virtues, say:
Come to me all you virtues,
And I will nourish you until the last drachma is asked for
And until the happy crowning of perseverance takes place.

The answer of the Virtues:
O glorious queen and most sweet mediatress,
we come to you freely.

Humility:
For that reason, most beloved daughters,
I will keep you in the royal bedchamber.
O daughters of Israel,
God aroused you under a tree
Wherefore at this time remember your own branches.
Rejoice therefore, daughter of Zion.
Hildegard Von Bingen's Mystical Visions page. 382-389
Vision Thirteen (1995)

I decided to stop meditating for a week and concentrate solely on reading this book of Dr Milanovich that Ann had given to me. It was a cleansing time for me and I felt able again to send healing out, as I was guided to do at the beginning of my journey.

I was sent some very important messages through my dreams, telling me, that, over the last few months, I had been in a state of empowering myself and increasing my spiritual abilities at a rapid rate. But without having experiences, knowledge, understanding and wisdom, I was compromising the all. I didn't want to be like rocky soil, where seeds grow very fast but the roots are shallow and easily eradicated, or like a seed that had fallen in the midst of thorns and once grown had been choked. I viewed myself in these two scenarios; if I was to carry on and force myself into this state of self-empowerment without any real understanding and knowledge, I risked feeding my ego (represented by the snake)into being driven by emotions and thoughts which were contrary to the will of our Father God. So, instead, I chose to sow my seeds deeply in a good soil and feed them with Patience and Faith hoping to gather the rewarding fruits, and waiting for Knowledge and Understanding to spring up delivering me Wisdom.

I understood one thing, God is pleased when we self-realise ourselves and learn by our own experiences in order that we absorb our lessons well and never have to be taught them again. Unconsciously, I had accepted the challenge of my test of initiation, even though I didn't know about the existence of such tests per se.

My prayers for guidance had been acknowledged by God and He decided to show me His Realms and His Infinity, to stimulate me. Now was time for me to prove myself through faith, hope and love, I needed to make myself worthy and learn my lessons, deserve to move forwards and have access to the higher realms. I needed to carefully coltivate this field and make sure the seeds never go dry. I needed to invest in it to make sure these seeds grow stronger and taller, and that the roots are anchored staidly into the ground, so I could give my share to the nations in times of their need.

Chapter 13

Initiation Tests

After my recent experience I began to appreciate more the responsibility that coming with my gift and be willing accept them so I might serve. Things changed during this time in several ways. I was changing my mode of meditation; I added new Guides and Archangels on my invocations, directing my attention first to my Guides, Archangels together with the Animals Spirits, Jesus and God Himself. Definitely, I was reaching a different dimension than before with the energies around me now being lighter, less dense and, in some cases, colder. The light I was seeing with my inner eye was from orbs, thresholds and the suns, and was very bright and sustainable, I discovered it was affecting my mental, emotional and physical states. I felt, and saw miracles in each meditation, in return I had to be more conscious of both my thoughts, (controlling them every moment of my daily life) and also my emotions, whenever I found myself in tense situations. I was being subjected to a real test and, at first it was very hard for me not to react in the wrong manner. I sometimes felt and saw a massive burning fire deep within my Sacral and Solar Plexus chakras when I was put under these intense tests.

"Love your brother/sister like your soul, protect that person like the pupil of your eye."
Saying 25 – Nag Hammadi Scriptures Gospel of Thomas by Marvin Meyer
(2007).

Some of my tests were made in such a way that I felt humiliated with my life and personality being torn apart. I was challenged all the time and instead of reacting as I normally would, I gave thanks for this opportunity to learn to be stronger. I learned to be calm and strong, and to not let things hurt me. I learnt on these occasions to give love instead of anger and hate.

"I will pay to no man the reward of evil. I will pursue him with goodness for the judgement of the Living is with God. And it is who will render to man his reward. I will not envy in a spirit of wickedness, my soul shall not desire the riches of violence." (Dead Sea scroll).

I learnt not to judge the behaviour of my fellow bothers and sisters out to see our efforts to survive and to do our best in our own ways to reach a state of safety and comfort. I needed to make a clear choice and statement that the most important thing in my life is God - God is Everything. This encouraged me to open more to my feminine side the one that is letting the universe come into me, rather than forcing things with my masculine side. I embraced not only the old wisdom, understanding and knowledge, but also the infinity above all prejudices.

I recognised the presence of our Living God who is present within (microcosms) and without (macrocosms), in every breath of our physical life. I understood the power of prayer, mantra, meditation, affirmations, our words, emotions and thoughts. This was for me a period of profound self-discovery, and no longer felt a need for a guru, master, or a life coach. I discovered my own guru and masters within myself and I was trusting them, empowering the little voice inside me. I employed discernment whenever I was listening to my inner voice or intuition carefully pondering the guidance and decisions, because we must remember that the deceiver is also inside us and he is able to mask himself and lead us astray. Finally I realised the meaning of the snake and who it is! I had lived and dealt with my devil every day, and to weaker that devil I must love my enemies like my friends. My goal is the Light and I was prepared to embark on my journey and fight as necessary.

I had another important dream/vision when did happened, I saw as a nightmare and disturbing, initially I was not going to include it in this book, but then when I unveiled its meanings, I understood it needed to be included, despite the fact was returning and bothering me until I decided to include into this book!

I was taken to a dark place out in the universe and found myself confronted with an ugly monster resembling a massive and savage bear in chains held by angels. Between myself and the bear there was what resembled a counter-balance scale with two seats placed opposite each other and a hanger on top. I was told to sit on one of the seats and the massive bear sat on the other infront of me. To my surprise, as we sat down my weight was far greater than that of the bear, I descended the bear shot up and I watched as his head was crushed by the top of the scales.

And I saw how those who had offered their souls for the glory of Lucifur
were judged in the scales of the heavenly weights and measures.
The black horse comes to judge those who are not prepared for the harvest
and the angels who are cast down from the higher heavens into bodies of
grottesquerie. They are weighed with the good seed and are revealed as the
seeds of Lucifur that had not borne heavenly fruit and could not be gathered
with the denarius of the Christ.
Each was measured according to his worth like a flower on the branches of
the Tree of Life in the days of the last-fruits.
The book of knowledge: The keys of Enoch keys 307:57-59 by Dr J J
Hurtak

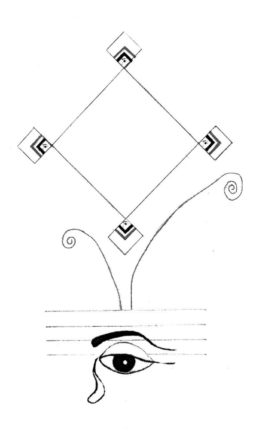

Prayer for Deliverance

For no worm thanks Thee, nor a maggot recounts Thy loving-kindness.
Only the Living thank Thee, all those whose feet totter, thank Thee, when Thou
makest known to them Thy loving-Kindness, and causest them to understand Thy
righteousness.
For the soul of all the living in Thy hand, Thou Hast given breath to all flesh.
O Lord, do towards us according to Thy goodness, according to the greatness of Thy
mercies, and according to the greatness of Thy righteous deeds.
The Lord listens to the voice of all who love his name and does not permit his lov-
ing-kindness to depart from them.
Blessed be the Lord, doer of righteous deeds, who crowns his pious ones with loving-
kindness and mercies.
My soul shouts to praise Thy Name, to praise with jubilation Thy Mercy,
To announce Thy faithfulness; there is no limit to Thy praises.
I belonged to death because of my sins, and my iniquities had sold me to Sheol.
But Thou didst save me, O Lord, according to the greatness of Thy mercies, according
to the greatness of Thy righteous deeds.
I, too, have loved Thy Name, and have taken refuge in Thy shadow.
When I remember Thy power, my heart is strengthened and I rely on Thy mercies.
Forgive my sins, O Lord, and purify me of my iniquity.
Grant me a spirit of faithfulness and knowledge; let me not be dishonoured in ruin.
Let not Belial dominate me, nor an unclean spirit; let pain and the evil inclination
not possess my bones.
For Thou, O Lord, art my praise, and I hope in Thee every day.
My brethren rejoice with me and the house of my Father is astounded by Thy gra-
ciousness.
......for ever I will rejoice in Thee.

Vermes, G., The Complete Dead Sea Scrolls in English Revised Edition, Penguin
Books, London, 2004, Dead Sea Scroll Hymns and Poems, Page 310-311.

Chapter 14

Uncovering The Universal Laws

The imperical ideology that I grasped during my reading was that energies, cannot be destroyed, only transformed. Based on this principle I learnt the four ways in which we interact with these energies - through our **Thoughts, Emotions, Words, and Actions; and all the energies move in a circular fashion!**

From reading the book *"The Light Set You Free"* by Dr Norma Milanovich and Dr Shirley D. McCune (1997), I got this knowledge, which helped me to put everything into perspective. This book also gave me the understanding of the Universal Laws. These Laws are part of what is called Hermetic wisdom, and they govern all the universes and planes of existences meaning that we are directly under their influences. These Universal Laws are not the same laws that we find in either our ancient or modern civilizations which were created to ensure an orderly society, nor are they religious or cultural laws from the ancient past which, if you did not respect them, you would be judged and punished.

"it was not through law that Abraham and his offspring received the promise that he would heir of the world, but through the righteousness that comes by faith. For if those who live by law are heirs, faith has no value and the promise is worthless,

because law brings wrath. And where there is no law there is no transgression. Therefore, the promise comes by Faith, so that it may be by Grace and may be guaranteed to all Abraham's offspring – not only to those who are of the law but also to those who are of the Faith of Abraham. He is the father of us all. As it is written: I have made you father of many nations – he is our father in the sight of God in whom he believed – the God who gives life to the dead and calls things that are not as though they were."
Romans 4:13-17 Holy Bible

"His followers said to him, who are you to say these things to us? You do not know who I am from what I say to you. Rather, you have become like the Jewish people, for they love the tree but hate its fruit, or they love the fruit but hate the tree."
Saying 43 – Nag Hammadi Scriptures Gospel of Thomas by Marvin Meyer (2007).

"What, then, was the purpose of the law? It was added because of transgressions until the Seed to whom the promise referred had to come. The law was put into effect through angels by a mediator. A mediator, however, does not represent just one party; but God is one. Is the law, therefore opposed to the promise of God? Absolutely not! For if a law had been given that could impart life, then righteousness would certainly have come by the law." Galatians 3:19-21.

These Laws are the laws of the Universe of higher realms as well as the lower realms that most of us do not acknowledge. These Laws are one with Faith and they are applicable through our Will.

"We will reap what we have sown, what goes around comes around."

These Universal Laws have been left by Hermes Trismegistus or Thoth the Egyptian God of Wisdom for humanity.

In this book I was reading these Laws were written through the channelling of Dr. Norma Milanovich from Ascended Masters, which confirmed to me the existence of Higher Intelligence and Realms beyond ours. They try to guide us to the higher truths, which are essential for our future.

Reading these laws, I was able to feel their vibrations via the channelled words. Every time I was reading a text transmitted by the Ascended Masters Kuthumi, El Morya or Jesus, I felt a strong connection through my third eye. I could feel their energies through the written text by reading with my mind and retaining them within my thoughts, thus accelerating the spin of my molecules. The more frequently I read this book the more I discover new part of My Self. I experimented by applying some of these laws to my daily life, and to my surprise they were working. I was using the *Law of Perpetual Transmutation of Energy* as my secret daily weapon and it helped on many occasions. I knew, above all else to monitor and control my thoughts, emotions, words and actions, because I was aware of their energies and how they could effect my life. All this gave me more confirmation about the world that, so far, I had seen only in my visions.

I was now able to relax and slow down my mental activities and emotions; letting the universe come to me once more. My mind was being stimulated and renewed at this time. I started to be inspired by the book and began to have thoughts like this one:

Everything moves as circular motion; we start from the atom, cells, all creatures living on Earth, Earth itself, Our Solar System, Our Constellation, Our Galaxy, All the Universe, and each one of them is separated by a membrane which embraces its own reality. These membranes are the barrier that separate one reality to another. Each reality has a different vibration frequency; each one of them has its own intelligence, which is based on the vibration frequency it lives on. The only thing motivated them is their will to complete a mission, and even though their will might appear different from each other, on the whole it is for the sustaining of the whole essence, and even though each one is separated by these membranes because of the different vibration energies residing in them, they are co-related, they are all one from the micro to the macro; we are all contributing to the creation of this universe.

Then I started to understand the origin of chaos which defines where we live.

Our life is like the little atom moving inside a cell around and around in a circular way, it is put in motion by his will to complete a given mission. There are other atoms that move in the same way with a different circular path and they are also put in motion by their will to complete the given missions. Then some of them start to think they are better than the others, that they should get more - they should have priorities or a better circular route, so they start to invade the spaces of each other (ego), and instead of working together for the good of all, they start to work for themselves. And this is the beginning of the clash, of competition, and survival behaviour becomes our priority. Here we manifest our aggressiveness, the masculine energies, resulting in fights and war. Some lose their track; others get confused. Some believe this circular path does not make any sense anymore and go in their own way and belief, while some give up completely. Only a few stick to the plan, so a dysfunctional system is created, which will eventually make the cell membrane collapse. This is the disease we call "cancer". The universal laws remain unchanging. They are untouchable, unbendable, and are the ones that eventually overrule the individual and will bring balance again to the all.

Chapter 15

The Chakra System

A couple years ago I didn't know anything about our chakras, but then I started to understand their importance for our evolution. These vortexes of energies are truly a micro-solar system, in which each one of them has a purpose, a vibration of frequency, and a consciousness. They both affect and are affected by our thoughts, emotions, words and actions in the way we live our life on the daily basis. They determine our energy system and are the key to our evolvement. I learnt some of the characteristic of each one of them. Through my meditation, I worked with all seven on a daily basis and I started to get a closer understanding of how they work and their importance.

The ancient awareness of the chakras come from Eastern cultures and however in the West, where most people have been influenced by the thought forms of traditional western religions that do not accept the existence of the chakras in our body, many have opened themselves to being more aware of their influences and powers, although most still remain ignorant of their significance. In the last thirty years the West has been flooded with books about the seven chakras system, and now of course people need only to tap into the internet to find out more about the chakras. For me, there is no spiritual evolvement without accepting and understanding the existence and the role of our chakras; they are an inherent part of us. I feel that my chakras are mini-reactors of energies, and in order for me to be in line and at one with the universe within and outside my essence, my chakras need to work together at full speed. When they are in harmony with each other the emanation of all seven colours are intensely clean and bright.

For the readers who are new to this, I will give just a brief explanation. Actually there are many chakras, but the most influential are the seven chakras that are critical to us in our daily life; they determine how we live our daily life depending on which chakra we are using during our daily routines. although there are others that start to be activated once one embarks on the spiritual path, the main seven are located along our spinal column binding our soul and aura to our physical body (our three-dimensional vehicle), keeping everything together. They transport, transmute, store, irradiate, release, and create energies around our body and beyond. In the western traditions old scriptures they are recognised as "Seals" and are mentioned in the Bible in the Revelation, "The Lamb opening of the seven Seals".

And they sang a new song:
'You are worthy to take the scroll and open its seals,
Because you were slain,
And with your blood you purchased man for God
From every tribe and language and people and nation.
You have made them to be a kingdom and priests to serve God, and they will reign
on the earth.'
5:9-10 Revelation Holy Bible

Each chakra radiates with a different frequency and has a different consciousness from each other. Those with the lower frequencies are the densest and slowest, whereas those with the higher frequencies are lighter and fastest.

The first Chakra- called the Base Chakra - is located between the legs and is connected to our gonads. Very dense and related to our instinct, it is our survival chakra and here we find our animal nature - our fight or flight reactions. Its colour is red, and it is the one that keeps us aligned and grounded with Mother Earth. Normally it is like a cone with a bigger opening looking down towards Mother Earth. This chakra must be also directly aligned with the Crown chakra, the one on top of our head, permitting the flow of all the energies in our chakras system along our spinal column.

The second chakra, the Sacral Chakra, is located just below our belly button, and is related to our sexual organs. Its colour is orange, and it spins faster than the Base Chakra. This chakra stores our emotions; it is the chakra of the duality of good and bad. I believe this chakra is one to watch when we find ourselves involved in unbalances or disagreements within or without. Normally, this is where the problem starts. This chakra is the one that prepares us with the tools to fight or flee after the first chakra, by influencing our minds and emotions to the possibilities of any particular outcome. Between this chakra and the third eye, they are all shaped in a double cone, all pointing toward one another with the larger parts looking out to the front and the back. (see diagram page 92)

The third chakra is located in the solar plexus area. This chakra burns yellow with the power to transform the energies from the chakra below and recycle them to be used by all of the other chakras. If the first chakra says to fight or flee, the second chakra starts to build the trenches and explore in depth the fight or flight strategies, so creating a plan. This third chakra is the supplier of the energies to fight or flee, or to let this energy be used for the above chakras. When the solar plexus is healthy this chakra spins at a faster rate than the one below, an influencing the adrenal glands which stimulate the production of hormones and adrenaline within our body.

The fourth or Heart Chakra is positioned as the name suggests, in the middle of our chests. It is a balancing chakra and it refines the energies coming from above and below where they are combusted by the solar plexus. The heart chakra uses these energies to transport it to wherever it is needed within our body similar to our physical heart pumping blood. This chakra for me is the singular most important chakra needed to balance our essence; it is the source and the producer of unconditional love, which releases us from all the binding and limitations. Within this chakra lie the mysteries that set us free when it is fully aligned with the Crown chakra. If the chakra is not functioning properly we will have difficulty in opening and working with the crown chakra, and we will be under the control of our ego, which manipulates our decisions and keeps our minds in a limited state of

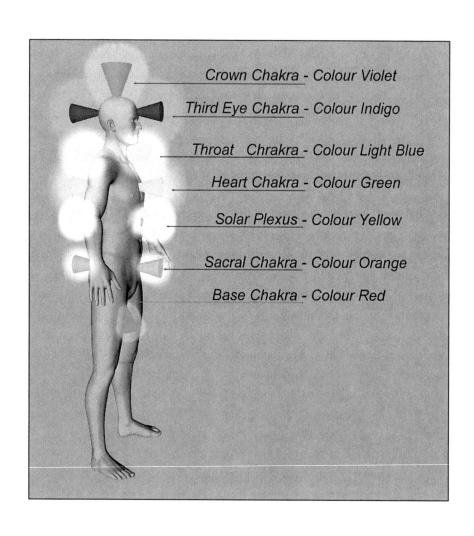

Crown Chakra - Colour Violet

Third Eye Chakra - Colour Indigo

Throat   Chrakra - Colour Light Blue

Heart Chakra - Colour Green

Solar Plexus - Colour Yellow

Sacral Chakra - Colour Orange

Base Chakra - Colour Red

consciousness! It is the heart chakra, which I believe our enemies try to destroy! Now, if the three chakras below are reacting, pondering planning and giving the strength for a war or flight, the flowing heart chakra, is the one asking, 'Why do we have the need to destroy and dissipate all our energies, when we can use them to create and help others. The opening and the functionality of this chakra is very important because it will align with the above chakras, linking all together and creating balance within and without of our essence. Its colour is green, and it influences the thymus gland. responsible for producing white cells and hormones for our body immune system. The heart chakra is know as the regulator chakra. When there are energies coming from above or downloading the heart chakra is the one that needs to ensure these energies are being absorbed into all of our essence. In fact, if it is not working properly it will create a blockage. I used to experience a heavy pressure in my chest and back after downloads because I was not focusing strongly enough on my heart chakra to let these energies be shared in all my essence. The energies were blocked at the heart level. Only when I started to use my heart more did the energies start to flow more freely.

The fifth or Throat Chakra is positioned in the middle of our throat and controls the talkative energies. It has influence over our thyroid gland. The thyroid glands control how quickly our body uses energy and produces proteins and hormones, regulating our metabolism.

Light blue in colour, when the energies coming from above pass through this chakra, these energies empower our words by giving them a higher vibrational energy enabling sound and light to become one, which I believe is where the power of manifestation can be achieved

"In the beginning was the Word and the Word was with God, and the Word was God." John 1:1 Holy Bible.

Words come out of our mouths and this is the chakra that allows whatever there is within, whatever comes from outside, whatever comes from below and whatever comes from the heights to interact with our present world reality. This is the chakra that becomes very active when we journey into other dimensions. When this chakra works properly we emanate through our words what is residing in us and what has been channelled through us. It influences all of the outer universe.

"Jesus said to them: if you fast, you will bring sin upon yourselves, and if you pray, you will be condemned, and if you give to charity, you will harm your spirits. When you go into any region and walk through the countryside, when people receive you, eat what they serve you and heal the sick among them. For what goes into the mouth will not defile you; rather it is what comes out of your mouth that will defile you."
Saying 14 – Nag Hammadi Scriptures Gospel of Thomas by Marvin Meyer (2007).

The sixth Chakra – the Third Eye – is located in the middle of the forehead. When activated it emits a pressure and irradiation of light; it influences the pituitary gland which is connected with the hypothalamus gland at the base of our brain. This gland produces many types of hormones and it has many functions such as: our growth, blood pressure, it plays a key role on pregnancy, our sensual organs, osmo-regularity, temperature regulations and many others role that scientist are beginning to discover. This chakra is associated with our left eye through this chakra we are enabled to see and feel the invisible. It is a very powerful chakra and can regulate and command all the other chakras below. It manifests within and it can manifest without.

"The Father that looks within and the Son that look without".

Its colour is indigo. For us to complete our full evolution the third eye must follow the guidance of the seventh chakra – the Crown – whilst being connected to the heart chakra because, if not, it will again be manipulated by the ego, which will creating more imbalances to sabotage our life.

"God has not created our universe in Six days but in Seven days He has created the all".

The seventh, or 'Crown' Chakra is located in the centre of our head and when fully developed it allows us to live in "Oneness" by receiving higher energies from above – energies which are then distributed to all of our body. The development of this chakra, together will all the other chakras below, allow us to integrate our life into the higher spiritual realm. It controls the upper brain and right eye, the pineal gland where the functions of which are still not clear to science, but I believe it can change our DNA and RNA coding. It has been written that this gland is very active and bigger in size from when we are infants age, but then it starts to shrink, calcify and become inactive, although recent experiments show that when this gland is exposed to light it starts to became active once again produces new types of hormones.

Again this chakra, violet in colour opens us to the outer universe from the eighth chakra and above. The aim of all of us is to be able to work with our crown chakra at all times and be one with all the chakras above in order to be in "Oneness" with our God. When we activate this chakra it resembles having a crown on our head.

Why are the chakras so important? We are been sealed off from the higher consciousness and these seals are the chakras! They are the holders of our inner consciousness, keeping the inner separate with the outer, with our energy field acting as a membrane. Every time we make a decision in our life, or those we have already made in our past lives, are directly connected with our inner energies thus enabling these energies to be regulated by the chakras and to change - by expanding or retracting based upon on our acts. Every time a scenario is presented into our life and we need to step forward to make a decision, we have an opportunity to change our inner energies, and by making the right move, we make our inner energies increase, expanding our energy field or light body. This reduces the gaps between us and higher intelligences bringing us a step closer to God, and letting us see the world in different way. If the opposite occurs, we go back or remain stuck in these illusions of good and evil *The Law of Polarity- Universal Laws*, and similar events re-occur until we have learnt our lessons.

As I have mentioned before, there are forces that do not want us to progress or increase our energy and vibrations. These forces control and manipulate our bottom three chakras. They are always there ready to steal from us, and keep us trapped in a lower state of mind, within these three chakras.

"But I tell you who hear me: Love your enemies, do good to those who hate you. Bless those who curse you, pray for those ill-treat you. If someone strikes you on one cheek, turn to him the other also. If someone takes your cloak, do not stop him from taking your tunic. Give to everyone who ask you, and if anyone takes what belongs to you, do not demand it back. Do to others as you would have them do to you. If you love those who love you, what credit is that to you? Even sinners love those who love them. And if you do good to those who are good to you, what credit is that to you? Even sinners do that. And if you lend to those from whom you expect repayment, what credit is that to you? Even sinners lend to sinners, expecting to repay in full. But love your enemies, do good to them, and lend to them without expecting back. Then your reward will be great, and you will be sons of the Most High, because he is kind to the ungrateful and wicked. Be merciful, just as your Father is merciful." Luke 6:27-36 Holy Bible.

Only when we start to move our attention to our heart chakras and we act within the 5th and 6th and the 7th chakras are we able to confront these tempters but without the help of the Most High we would not have a chance to overcome them. Therefore prayers and praises are important as we need to learn to pray and rely on Faith asking for forgiveness and repentance so that we may receive the help we require to win this battle.

The understanding of the chakras, leads also to understand life in the universe. We are creators of energies, and we need to make sure that we produce good energies.

The colours of these chakras are the same as the colours of the rainbow and when they are all in agreement, the sum of all of them produces white light in the same way that our eyes see the seven colours of rainbow light which normally are encompassed within white light.

When I fed my chakras through my meditation/visualization sessions, I was always aware of their energies. When I had blockages I would notice them straight away because of the uncomfortable sensations I experienced in a particular area. I would say from my experience and from all the spiritual courses I have done, Usui Reiki is the one that made me work straight away with the chakra system. However, without the Munay Ki I would never have understood the true meaning and power of the chakras. Through the feeding of my seeds of Munay Ki, which were placed into my chakras, I was able to explore the difference of each one of them, and this also helped me to meditate on them and understand the power of the colours. I also believe that no course is better than the other but rather it is the unity, of the different techniques, belief and understandings that makes the totality, and this is what I am trying to achieve within this chapter. All is One and One is the All. We need to be aware of our chakra system as part of our essence as within it lie the initial keys of human evolution.

Chapter 16

The Promise – The Holy
Spirit and The Golden Temple

By now it must have been six months since my awakening, and I was studying
many books and having dreams containing important underlying meanings vital
to my spiritual path. I was aware of their significance and so I started to keep a
diary of them, trying to interpret them based on my current knowledge. Some I
could decipher whilst others I had difficulty with.

I was after the messages that my guides were trying to tell me about.
Sometimes the scenario of a dream would change but the message was still
the same. I had dreams that told me to empower myself and listen to my
feminine side *(the Law of Gender - Universal Laws, right side of our brain)*. They
were telling me to let my feminine side come forward because, although I
was slowly changing both my way of meditation and my way of thinking, I
was still using visualization and thus forcing myself to be rational and analytical
(masculine part of us, left side of our brain). My dreams were telling me I
needed to trust the messages coming to me. Several of my dreams were about
other tests that I needed to pass in order to forge ahead. There is no point in
describing and explaining each dream here, what I want to emphasise that
the messages were clear and, when I did not understand fully, they returned
with different scenarios.

My inner self was being challenged every day and my aim was to master
and control my emotions and my thoughts, I was required to be able to

forgive easily, to be humble, to be more understanding, to be compassionate, to give love in a situation where I would previously have given anger or hate.

"Hate does not stop with hate, but hate does stop with Love"

"Do not judge, and you will not be judge. Do not condemn, and you will not be condemned. Forgive, and you will be forgiven."
Luke 6:37 Holy Bible

When my mind was free of any earthly entanglement I was subjected to these tests and as I was being challenged with very intense scenarios so I was trying to control the situation with my mind and as a result I was experiencing a burning fire within my stomach. All of this would be energy that previously I would have wasted through my hot-tempered reactions. Previously I used to hang on to these damaging negative thoughts and emotions for days and even weeks. They used to exhaust me by draining my energies thereby lowering my vibration and keeping me in a lower state of mind. In other words I was being mentally robbed. When I recognised this fact and no longer let them rob me in this way, I was able to see what was happening here. These thoughts and emotions or energies were been combusted by my solar plexus chakra and then re-used to increase my overall vibration. I used to have all sorts of thoughts and emotions, they were coming to me at any time in the day and night and these were trying to mislead and deceive me by creating fear, anger, and insecurity within, but by following my inner guidance, which was telling me to react differently and remain calm and tolerant at all times, I learnt to thank these thoughts and emotions for coming to me, bless and release them into the Light. If they would not go I embraced them with pink, blue, violet and white light depending how upon I was feeling at that moment and watched them dissolve in the Light.

When I was being tested by other people I also used this technique and surrounded my self with white light projecting a pink or violet light into the other person *(The Law of Transmutation - The Universal Laws)*. My aim was to dissolve the negativities and it was working! Slowly, partly by following my dreams and inner guidance and partly by understanding and applying the Universal Laws, I emerged from this stormy situation. I remembered the teaching of Jesus when he said, 'If your enemy slaps you in one side of the cheek, give the other cheek.' and I understood that if I reacted in this way, this enemy was giving me the opportunity to learn to go forward therefore not getting trapped in the vicious circle *(Law of Cause and Effect - The Universal Laws)*. Jesus with His sayings was teaching us to control our emotions, thoughts, words and action. The result was that, instead of being sad, I was happy to find myself in these circumstances. Without them I never would have understood the influences of my ego, or the outer forces over me. I would not know that there is a part within me that is controlling these thoughts and emotions which are not mine. I could now control and transform them and found that more I was doing this the easier it was becoming. This process and experience signified the beginning of me gaining control of my lower self. Together with the use of the mantras and affirmations I was saying everyday, I always kept myself open and in a positive state of mind, thus creating ever more protection around me. It was after these events that I started to have better control of myself -I started to experience something new again!

One afternoon, I was nearly at the end of feeding all of my chakras when I started to have visions. In the past months I'd had visions, during my soul journeying but they were triggered by me visualising first and then letting the universe guide me where I needed to go. This time it was very different; I was not expecting or trying to visualise or journeying but these visions came to me on their own accord. When I started to focus my attention on them I saw something truly extraordinary. When I reached the rites of earth keeper, the visions started to come, and they became steadily more intense and clear. I did not stop feeding my rites and chakras but carried on until the end and, when I reached my crown chakra I started to go through to other dimensions. I felt something was pressuring me to finish my meditation, but I chose to carry on. I saw colour and stars and planets were all moving I was travelling towards them. Suddenly I saw a quadrant of beings marching in armour like in a big cubic golden formation, all moving along in unison as marching into a battle (I understood these were the Hosts of Light) I saw various strange shapes, many of them, and then it all happened. I went through a very bright light and my third eye was flashing white light. It was so very intense that I could not see through it at first, but eventually I went through an open golden door, which overlooking the darkness beyond. I entered the doorway where it was very dark at first, but then I saw a blue-white Flame in front of me and within its bright deep blue centre, burned a big blue Flame. In a split second I suddenly knew what I was seeing as I saw it in Its splendour. It was the Holy Spirit! I said, 'I am a servant.' And I bowed my head in a sign of respect.

I saw that the Holy Spirit was expanding and contracting as if it was breathing, but there was no sound; I could not hear anything, even though for a minute I thought it was speaking to me. Appearing next was what I thought at first to be an angel-like shape, but rather they were symbols and figures - gifts for me that I took, eyes closed, with my hand I brought them into my heart chakra. While I was putting them into my heart chakra so more gifts were coming and I could feel the energies in my hands. As I gave my thanks the story of Parsifal came into my mind still the gifts kept flowing. When I felt and saw that the gifts had finally stopped coming, I knew it was time for me to withdraw, so I left through the same door as I had entered. It was all so beautiful; I was filled with such of joy I only wished it could have lasted longer!

When I came back within myself, I could not believe what had just happened. I was ecstatic, but reluctant to tell others about this experience as I feared that they would not believe me and I didn't want appear a fantasist. I decided to keep it to myself for a while, until I felt confident enough to speak about it to other people.

This vision was the beginning of many esoteric gifts and symbols received by me during my meditations over the period of several months. I was even instructed to draw some of the gifts and symbols.

These symbols are part of the language of Light, we absorb them into our essence and their purpose is to empower our Higher Selves, which in turn use His fight to transmute and anchor the Light of our Most High in other dimensions. I was told to keep the images I had drawn, so I did.

One morning, I awoke early but, as I was feeling very tired and sleepy, I thought I would rest for another hour or so before getting up. I started

"In the last days, God says: I will pour out my Spirit on all the people. Your sons
and daughters will prophesy, your young men will dream dreams.
Even on my servants, both men and women, I will pour out my Spirit in those days,
and they will prophesy.
I will show wonders in the heaven above and signs on earth below, blood and fire
and billows of smoke. The sun will be turned to darkness
and the moon to blood
before the coming of the great and glorious day of the Lord.
And everyone who calls on the Name of the Lord will be saved."
Acts 2:17-21 Holy Bible.

grounding, which by now had been happening every morning for the last few days, and I found was also connecting with the energies above. The connection was getting ever stronger and soon I started to journey and have high celestial visions, while travelling to other worlds and crossing thresholds of energies and light. At one point, I came across a cascade of water, and was given access to a majestic temple or palace, which was enveloped in an aura of thin, golden light, standing before the entrance on the outside I saw two beings, who appeared to be the guardians of the place were placed one on each side of the entrance, I noticed they had small wings and were wearing suits of golden armour, there were Cherubim. I felt full of love as I ventured inside and found myself in this corridor that I walked along until I came upon a Golden Spirit. The atmosphere was full of love and all of the surrounding air was golden. During these visions a part of me acknowledged pressure to leave the place, but I knew I must stay as long as possible; it was the same part of me that had been urging me to abandon my meditation of three days earlier when I experienced the Holy Spirit. But I knew that this was Heaven, so I could not comprehend this sensation I spoke with the Golden Spirit, and He told me it is fine to feel like this. The beauty of this place was such that nobody would want to leave, I felt honoured and blessed to be there and I was worried to be seen as disrespectful, because I was tremendously fortunate to see what I was seeing, but again I had these thoughts of pressure to return to planet Earth. Reluctantly I left and came back to myself.

In the following days I felt most unwell, and suffered from flu like symptoms. I had been invited to participate in a workshop at the weekend and, despite my health condition, I chose to attend and was glad I did. The workshop included a spiritual atonement and, on this occasion my connection remained very strong. Every time I closed my eyes I was having visions, but I didn't want to draw any attention to myself. I was seeing a sea of Golden Light and I knew, if I would let myself, I could have strong visions while I was there, so instead I decided to stay with the group. I was not confident enough to let it go in front of others; I was too wary of them.

This course helped me to understand how easily each individuals vibration can be raised when they work together as a group. Group

"His followers said to him, 'When will the rest for the dead take place, and when will the new world come?' He said to them, 'What you look for has come, but you do not know it.' "

Saying 51 - Nag Hammadi Scriptures Gospel of Thomas by Marvin Meyer (2007).

meditations, even simple ones like: the Mahatma Energies Meditation, or the Pillar of Light Meditation become very powerful. (Anyone could attain these meditations through the internet to complete one of this meditation will require an half hour of your time). It was an important exercise to work in a group for me, because I had been on my own since the beginning of my awakening and this enabled me to appreciate how in unison we could reach a high state of mind much easier than acting alone.

"The purpose of the Cherubim is to create a wall of Light around the 'Specific Plan' being used to connect worlds of generation and generation. They insure that the thought-forms of the Masters and ascended Masters are "perfectly consistent" with the Father's Plan in perfecting the number of Souls destined to share in a creative Plan."
The Book of Knowledge: Keys of Enoch Key 303:79 by Dr. J J Hurtak

Because of my lack of understanding and knowledge, I did not get to know the meaning of all these happenings. Only in my later stage I comprehended who allowed me to travel in spirit - the Seraphim and Ophanim. From this time on, all my readings were being guided, and I was guided to read it only when the time was right for my consciousness to absorb it and learn.

If I had read some of the books before my experiences, my mind would have tried to block or sabotage them, and make the reality appear as a result of my imagination! Because I had visions, dreams and saw what I saw with my own eyes <u>before</u> I read any books confirming my experiences. I <u>knew</u> they were real.

Chapter 17

Soul Journeying – the beginning of transmutation

After the recent workshop I began to amalgamate the things I learnt with Reiki and the ones I learnt with Munay Ki, plus the reading I was doing. I changed part of my invocation to create a sacred place by adding other Ascended Masters and Archangels and quickly I noticed the difference, the energies in my space were stronger than before. Jesus was and is my main Guide, but from time to time I was invoking the essences of Kuthumi and Lord Melchizedeck or all tree together to guide me. I believe, it was a phase of experimentation, trying new ways to meditate.

During all this time, I understood how effective is **the power of visualisation**! I remember when I first started I had some difficulty in visualising the Light, which I was using to feed my seeds within the chakras, but with practise and determination it was now becoming very easy to visualise this Golden Light and it got better when I used it in conjunction with my respiration; the Golden Light made the air we breathe become Manna or Prana, the Golden Light is Prana or Manna! And then I was bringing it into my body. I was testing which ways would be more beneficial for my essence to absorb the Light.

I was alternating my meditation with the journeying, and it was done by guidance in a random way. At times I was feeding my chakras and at other times I was journeying into other worlds. My guided journeying into other dimensions enabled me to receive the gifts from the Holy Spirit and through feeding my chakras I was keeping my vibration high enough to be able to journey to other dimensions.

At this time, I felt that all my commitment and determination had started to pay off. It was more than a pleasure for me to invest my time into meditation and journeying, and the more I was doing it, the more I understood this was the way, the right way for me to interact and receive higher intelligence "The Light".

Only by investing our time in meditations, prayers and praise can we get closer to the higher realities, otherwise we would be cut off and not know of their existences and it would remain beyond our imagination. Another thing I learnt was that if I had not written all of this in a diary, many of my experiences would have been forgotten. Although very real, these visions started to fade after a very short time, as they are not yet fitted to our three-dimensional consciousness. The reality where we currently live, acts as a barrier and will try to block and dissipate any kind of higher reality that we might experience.

Only through the high Wisdom man understand what he sees, and high Wisdom is reached through Faith; and true Faith is reached through Humility; and Humility is reached by Will, and all of them are reached through God by Prayers, Repentance, Praises, but first man need to understand and live in a complete Truth and try to find Peace with himself!

When, I was journeying or meditating I never went into a deep trance. I was always in touch with our Earthly reality so my whole essence was experiencing it. Through journeying, my soul was gathering experience of the existence of other realities, worlds, star systems and universes and when I watched some of the astronomy programmes they were transmitting to me a strong sense of limitations, entrapment in our three-dimension reality, after experiencing the limitless, all of our perceptions, understanding and explanation of our local universe seemed very limited. I felt so curtailed even watching it on TV - it was like watching unreachable, uncomprehensible and inaccessible realities, separated from our existence on planet earth. This is far from what I have experienced. Again, this is because we are trapped within a three-dimensional membrane and the reality within is dictated by our five senses and makes us believe this is the all, and that we are the only living creatures in this universe!

During my meditations I saw the battle of some forces, that were trying to keep me within the Third dimension limited state of mind. I was crossing into new dimensions of different beings that didn't want me to leave our three-dimensional consciousness of time and space. I was attacked psychically during my meditation by transgressions, thoughts, persistent earthly pressures, false duties and worries, creating a restless state of mind and making me believe I was wasting my time, and that all of this was not real. How do we know what is real or not real? Who can tell us if it is real or it is not real? Doctors? Clerics? Scientists? Do they have experience in these matters? In which theory or facts do we have to base our truths?

"Who knows everything but lacks of oneself, lacks everything"
Saying 67 – Nag Hammadi Scriptures Gospel of Thomas by Marvin Meyer (2007).

Luckily we are reaching a state of awareness. Nowadays it is easy to find proof, written in the present and also in the records of past events. Man is not only what anthropologists describe us as we are far more than that! This is my answer, but it does not mean that other theories or facts are wrong or there is only one truth. I believe there are many levels of truth but, like I mentioned earlier in the chakras chapter, it is influenced by which chakra consciousness we, as individuals, are living in our world. I believe also that we have been deprived and kept ignorant by forces trying to stop us fully realising ourselves, ones that do not want us to acknowledge the existence of other realities.

"Do not give what is holy to dogs, or they might throw them upon the manure pile.
Do not throw pearls to swine, or they might make mud of it." Saying 93 – Nag
Hammadi Scriptures Gospel of Thomas by Marvin Meyer (2007).

At the beginner of my journeying I used to battle with bad thoughts and ugly grotesque beings. I used to be deceived by these forces, which were trying to stop me proceeding with my spiritual studies. By undermining me, they tried to create confusion and frustration in order that I would react with my lower bodies. These are the physical, emotional and mental bodies - which are directly connected with the lower and denser chakras. They were trying to block the spinning of my chakras and the flow of energies and thus were encouraging me to commit an offence or a sin!

"Therefore do not let sin reign in your mortal body so that you obey its evil desires. Do not offer the parts of your body to sin, as instruments of wickedness, but rather offer yourselves to God, as those who have been brought from death to life; and offer the parts of your body to him as instruments of righteousness. For sin shall not be your master, because you are not under law, but under Grace. What then? Shall we sin because we are not under law but under Grace? By no means! Don't you know that when you offer yourselves to someone to obey him as slaves, you are slaves to the one whom you obey — whether you are slaves to sin, which leads to death, or to obedience which leads to righteousness?" Romans 6: 12-17 Holy Bible.

If we commit a sin or offence this stops us from indwellings with our higher truths by creating blockage within our chakras system. When I found myself making mistakes, I would not be able to experience or cope with the flow of energies within my body. I would be trapped within the reality in which we live daily, however I did not stop at the surface but was faithfully led guided and I relied on my Guidance. Eventually, after months of ups and downs (*The Rhythm of life – Universal Law*) , all of these negative energies were contained by learning how to transmute them. Now while all these thoughts and emotions were invading my mind with aim to create a reaction - and I needed to react because ignoring them would make their influences even stronger. I started to apply what I had learnt so far. I needed to **manifest the power of Love and Light in order to transform these thoughts and emotions** and my Higher Self knew exactly how to proceed.

In the higher Heavens The Father is Thought and Fire, The Mother is Emotion and Water and together both of them make Mind. The Son is conceived by Mind, He is Love, He is Air and The Word. If there is a Son surely there is a Daughter and She is represented by the Creators God The Elohim and all of them are Life or Living Light. In the lower heavens thought the father is a falsehood, the mother is corrupt, and the word the son is a blasphemy and the daughter is dead. But we have been saved. We have been given the Word from the Higher Heavens to resurrect the daughter from death to Life, reconnecting her with the true Father and Mother!

There was no more confusion or fear; my mind now understood that anger, hatred, fear and frustration would make them stronger; it is impossible to remove or destroy them as energies cannot be destroyed but only transmuted. So when new scenarios and visions were coming into my mind containing these negative thoughts and emotions, I started to transmute them with the power of Love and Divine Light and the result was so strong that it was affecting my emotional and mental states until they stopped bothering me.

These were all lessons I needed to learn. I was being put in a position to make decisions, some of which involved very violent scenarios created within my mind, coming to me in the form of visions, dreams and thoughts; trying to stimulate and picture me in these situations. I was being tested. I have been faced with creating new realities using the power of Love, Compassion and Peace, which are the virtues needed to transform the violent scenarios.

"The true salvation start from within ourselves"

"When you know yourselves, then you will be known and you will understand that you are children of the Living Father."
Saying 3:4 – Nag Hammadi Scriptures Gospel of Thomas by Marvin Meyer (2007).

The purpose of all this was to challenge me in order that I could proceed to the next step on my spiritual path; it was like training for an exam! These past months I had learnt the theory, but to apply it required strong will to manifest the power of Love. We have these tests daily in our earthly life, sometime we read, study and experience it, but then there comes a time when we need to apply what we have studied or experienced in order to master the situation and go further in our life. Very seldom do we apply what we have learnt, because our mind and emotions take over by reacting and controlling the course of events, so our soul never learns!

The Dead Sea Scroll speaks about three nets of Belial (Devil) to entrap men. These are **Fornication, Greed,** and **Profanation of the temple (God)**. Each one of us also has weak points and the devil within us knows which ones they are, and he will bring upon us situations or temptations in order to make us sin. And when we have been challenged we should be happy because we have been given an opportunity to overcome these obstacles and go further with our lives.

Often the person closest to us is used as an instrument to make us learn our lessons. Reacting badly, creating hate, anger, violence and fear is a sign that we are not ready to move forward, and being resentful or enable to forgive makes us slave of our opponent. Only by not keeping these bad feelings and thoughts will we manage to unbind ourselves from these chains *(The Law of Vibration - Universal Laws)*. With the gift of Forgiveness we free ourselves and no be enslave by these negativities anymore, and by using Unconditional Love and Compassion, we transmute them, and they became our strengths rather than our weaknesses. Finally we will have succeeded in overcoming the test and will be ready to face the next challenge.

"Why do you wash the outside of the cup? Do you not understand that one who made the inside is also the one who made the outside."
Saying 89 – Nag Hammadi Scriptures Gospel of Thomas by Marvin Meyer (2007).

"Whatever resides within determines what will appear and will be manifested outside."

Chapter 18

Experiencing Stonehenge and The Crop Circles

After a period of cleansing, I had been invited to join a group of ten people for a ceremony at Stonehenge on 3rd August and to investigate the energies in the famous crop circle formations. My friends Ann and Graham promised me that we would go together to see the crop circles in Wiltshire area after the ceremony. In the past I heard them speaking a lot about the crop circles, about the energies within the formations and the mysteries behind. There has been much discussion about them, about how they got there and who their creators are. Were they alien-made or man-made? After many years there are still a lot of speculation about these events. I was intrigued; I was curious as to what I could sense there, because of all my recent experiences of feeling and seeing. Finally, I was going to be in a place where thousands of people believe and feel the vibrations emanated by these crop formations which are not understood by most of us. I was also worried about disappointing my friends if I would not be able to perceive anything! I felt full of energies and also fortunate to have this opportunity to participate in such event at one of the most sacred site in Britain.

I set off later in the afternoon, after giving some healing to my partner, she was not feeling very well and I was amazed how much colour I could see clearly with my inner eye during the healing sessions.

I spent the night in hotel near Stonehenge where I was going to meet the rest of the group next morning I rose early, showered, then drove to the site of Stonehenge uncertain what to expect. When I reached the proximity of Stonehenge I could see clearly open fields and the hill where these sacred stones were placed, truly a majestic view. The morning sky was grey and drizzly with a little mist. I met up with my group and together we went towards the sacred stones. We had booked in advance so were allowed to go inside between the stones and Graham kindly explained to me the flow of energies among the stones. We formed a circle and each one of us had a copy of the prayer of the Great Invocation that Wendy one of the group had written. Her printed handout included our names in each sections of the prayer, to remind us who needed to recite what. When we prayed it was beautiful and very overwhelming; I was honoured to have been chosen to close the invocation, then a lady from another group of four individuals who were praying at another corner of the site started to sing in a language that we could not understand, but the sound was immensely haunting. Later she told us that she was singing in Aramaic an ancient language, spoken in the times of Jesus and before.

We went to have breakfast and I had a chat with Ann and Graham about our latest insights. It was interesting for me to share my experiences and points of view because, being on my own most of the time, I felt the need to share these thoughts and happenings.

Finally, we drove to the crop circle area in Wiltshire. Ann was not feeling very well and she stayed in the camper van, while Graham and I went to the café that is a meeting point for all the people who wish to find the locations of all the crop circles. In that season there had been about seventy formations and most of them were available for public access giving us the opportunity to see and feel their vibrations. Some of the shapes were symbols of sacred geometry and these pictures were displayed hanging on the walls of this café for anyone to see. I found it a fascinating place to be. Graham asked me which one I would be interested in seeing - a difficult decision to make as there were so many of them but while I was pondering the question, I heard a person behind us suggesting to his friends, to go and see the one which was a Yin and Yang formation which sounded like a good idea so I asked Graham that we should go and see that one. Based on this decision we chose other three formations in the vicinity of this Yin and Yang circle. Graham had plotted them on in his map, so we knew exactly where they were located, so I drove while he gave me directions and, before long we arrived at the first of these formations, I realised how big the fields were. It was raining but it amazed me, there was nobody else there.

Once inside the formation, we went with the flow of the energies and I could feel the vibrations constantly tickling in my hands. I stopped walking and let the energies flow into my body. I could not stand still due to the great strength of the energies which were making my body sway backwards and forwards. I was attuning with my eyes closed and seeing with my inner eye. There was an intense golden light and, from time to time, a flashing of green, some shapeless faces and I got the feeling that the aliens were there, watching us. It was wonderful sensation.

It was mid-afternoon before we finished in this formation so we chilled out for thirty minutes before moving on to the next site. which was also deserted. We went all around the formation, then I placed myself in the centre of the crop circle and started to attune myself with it. Again I saw a pink light, violet and green flashes all within a golden light; the spinning energies were increasing and Graham, who was standing behind me was telling me he was seeing gold too. The rush of energies were causing my body to pivot backwards and forwards, twisting me to one side in the same direction of the pull of the of energies being drawn into the formation. I had difficulty trying to remain still; my right hand was shaking uncontrollably and my body was fighting to cope with these extreme higher energies, when alien faces materialised before me through my inner eye, emerging from the golden Light. The faces were similar to those I had seen before – big black rhomboid eyes in an oval shaped head with a pointed chin; everything was enveloped in a bright golden glow.

It finally dawned on me where all our creative imaginations of sci-fi films were gaining their inspiration from! We may believe these images are merely creations of our imagination, but I had proof that day these images or beings that we create with our imagination really do exist and our sub-conscious self is aware of them, thus they became pigments of our imagination or fantasy world. These realities that at times our sub-conscious brings forward to our

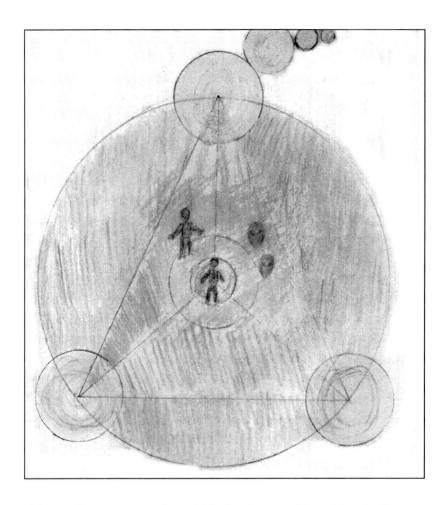

I believe that we are part of a multi-level universe, within an hierarchical system,
each one encompassing the one below. The one above can descend to the one below,
but the one below cannot go up unless they overcome the energy fields of the
membranes or thresholds. I also believe, this multi-level universe has been temporarily
cut off from the Master Tree, and this is the time for our reconciliation.

three-dimensional life sometime through art, paintings, films, books etc. and they can be good or bad images, all depending on which channel we have chosen or we have attached ourselves to! We humans have always known of the existence of other beings, the ones we call aliens, and many of us perceive them purely as result of our imagination but in truth they are real and very much active on our planet. From time to time people have seen them flying around a fact that it has been well confirmed and documented. There are many files with testimonials from government authorities and civilians that speak about them and on several occasions their appearance has been associated with attempts to stop us destroying our planet!

For me, my visit to Stonehenge and the crop circles was an eye-opening experience! I witness and confirm to you that, without a doubt, the crops circles are real! And they are made by beings of Light that we humans call Aliens. I could have stayed there for a very long time; there was a beautiful sensation of Love and Peace.

For years people have wanted to see these beings in the process of forming the crop circles, but they were either not there in time or close enough and I know why! We cannot see them with our physical eyes if they do not want to be seen. They live in a higher wave frequency, a different dimension where our human eyes cannot detect them. It is the same as ultraviolet light that we now know that exists but our eyes cannot see it without the use of a special machine to expose the light or adjust the frequency to the spectrum of our human eye in order to be visible to us.

After this experience, Graham told me that there are other places in this area that he wished to show me, but at the pace we were going, he didn't think we had enough time left. He took me to see a burial chamber dated 4000 BC, where to my surprise I detected strong energies too. While there, we had a strange encounter with a person who came rushing into the chamber, panting for breath. At first he remained silent, as though listening, and then he was shouting to another person outside who was speaking loudly on his mobile phone. He stormed out to him and told him to turn it off. Then, he re-entered the chamber, looked at us and smiled. When we were outside, admiring the yin and yang of the crop formation that laid in the field in front of us and the burial chamber, this person approached us, as if he wanted to have a chat. I told him that he should go to feel the energies in the formation below us, to my surprise he turned to me saying that humans make the crop circles and that they are fake! With that he turned away and strode off down the hill. It felt strange! Unfortunately it was time for me to return home but I promised myself a longer stay next year.

During my next meditation I was asking my guides questions about the crop circles and had a intense clear vision whereby I was journeying into other worlds which I believe was influenced by my time at the crop circles. The answers I received were: *the aims of the symbols of the crop circles is to balance and raise the vibration of this country, to give messages ahead to what is going to happen and within a symbol there is a great amount of intelligence and vibration which are absorbed by our human consciousness.*
Our brain is not developed enough to understand and comprehend the full meaning and effect that these symbols have both as individuals and on our entire planet.

After my visit to the crop circles, things really started to move on. Through my third eye I could see my hands becoming like beams of light feeding my chakras. I was guided to build a sacred area, which I could meditate within, so I printed pictures of my guides, which I felt a strong connection with and laminated a beautiful picture of a mix of Light which I saw as a creation point 'Source of the All,' placing it in the middle of my sacred altar. I was not using candles anymore to retrieve the light. Rather, I was invoking the Light from above and every time I opened my palms to receive the Light I could feel this Light flowing in my hands then flooding through my chakras into all my essence.

So yet again I was guided to change my routine. Some days I was feeding my rites and other days just soul-journeying, by visualizing myself going up through the Tree of Life, seeing the different levels and then, when I reached the 5th level, meeting with my Original Self and visualising us on merging as one. I was amazed how many orbs of Light or thresholds I used to see, and every time I went to places with a very strong Light my entire body was influenced by it, with beautiful sensations of Peace and Love.

Chapter 19

Unleashing The Spiritual Warrior

Since the crop circle experience I had a series of intense dreams and meditations session. Also I had times where I just could not connect or see the Light at all, riding the ups and downs of *The Law of Rhythms - Universal Laws*, and leaving me feeling a little unbalanced. What I knew for certain was that my dreams were trying to tell me something about near future events and external influences. I was guided to be attuned to Karuna Reiki, very different from Usui Reiki. It was another very interesting experience. I immediately felt the benefit of the energies that I got to know as highly intense feminine power of Quan Yin, which I believe aided my balance during this turbulent time. I saw her essence and decided to include her in my rituals and for the next seven days I absorbed her essence by putting each one of her symbol into my chosen chakras. As result of this action, in the following weeks I had strong downloads and clear visions containing geometrical figures. When I was closing my eyes, my third eye was flashing light and sometimes caused me headaches, so I was guided to rest and avoid meditating for a few of days.

Even though I only stopped meditating for a short while, I was aware of the negative effect on me. The harsh reality of the illusion in which we live was getting so strong that even with my profound faith my mind began to question everything and I risked letting my work so far, be forgotten, dissolved in the chaos of our time-space, as events purely the fruit of my imagination! As already mentioned in the past chapters, I devotedly kept a diary, a move I felt was vital to keep everything alive. Even after a strong vision or meditation I knew if I did not write them down, quickly my mind would scrutinise and try to dismiss everything as a pigment of my imagination. Leaving them to be forgotten over time.

In September, I was guided to finally read a book called – *'YHWH The book of knowledge: the Key of Enoch'* by Dr J J Hurtak. I was in Tanzania on holiday at the time, and digesting it made me contemplate in depth and give me the answer to my question, why humans are on Earth? By reading the Introduction of the book strong thoughts were flowing through me, they were about *the spiral shapes of the Universes, which are open ended and infinite.*

I learnt that we, the human race, have been placed here according to the plan of God to use planet Earth as an experiment, to create a stronger and more evolved stars system, this can be achieved by reinforcing the faith and character of souls through teaching us how to transform negative and low nature energies into the higher ones. The key to these teachings are encoded in these three words: Love, Light and Oneness. All of us have come from the stars, and into the stars we will return, in order to sustain the Light, which is required to create and recreate an infinite universes. On the night of the 29th September 2009 I had an incredible vision/experience; I was flying around different worlds and realities. I was dressed in silver armour, with a helmet and sword, ready for battle. I had little wings on my ankles; I was dressed like the mythological Greek god, Hermes and I was enforcing the will of God. I felt invincible and I could transmute anyone of lower nature by using the powers that we call Light and Love. Travelling at very high speed, I visited different worlds and realities, confronting different species of beings, transmuting them by using these energies of Light and Love, making them become part of the One. The emanation of these energies was extremely powerful. I met my Lord Jesus and I received his blessings and through the knowledge of the Universal Law to fight the forces of darkness. Nobody and nothing could resist the power of these energies coming out from my heart. I was transmuting many. I was in places where there was much darkness I was transmuting them into Light. Many beings tried to stop me, but they too were being transmuted, their opposition to the Light was useless, utterly impotent and they were easy to overcome. Then I found myself in a place rather like a tribunal room where souls standing in the middle were been judged, there were beings dressed in dark, a judge sitting in the same way our earth judges sits and some others holding the souls, this judge and the ones holding the souls had red eyes, same as the ones I saw in the first days of my awakening. I was trying to transmute with Light and Love all of them, the ones around and in front of me, including the judge. It was obvious that those beings standing in front of me were not very happy at my interference in their business, but I sensed that there were already aware of what was going to happen to them. They were not surprised to see me and did not try to resist me, but when I started to project Love and Light from the centre of my heart, two Angels came from above and picked me up and removed me from that place. Then, I came back into my earth sense again. Shocked, I asked myself, numerous questions; 'What was that? What was I doing there? Why had the angels removed me and stopped me transmuting? Again, I needed to find answers! I thought, maybe I was there by mistake?

This experience/vision was very meaningful. And it was again only later, after a year of studying looking for answers; I discovered the meaning of what I saw, in a book called Pistis Sophia!

"Now, therefore, if the time of that man is completed, first cometh forth the destiny and leadeth the man unto death through the rulers and their bonds with which they are bound through the Fate. And thereafter the retributive receivers come and lead that soul out of the body. And thereafter the retributive receivers spend three days circling round with that soul in all the regions and dispatch it to all the aeons of the world. And the counterfeiting spirit and the destiny follow that soul; and the power returneth to the Virgin of Light.

And after three days the retributive receivers lead down that soul to the Amente of the Chaos; and when they bring it down to the chaos, they hand it over to those who chastise. And the retributive receivers return unto their own regions according to the economy of the works of the rulers concerning the coming-forth of the soul.

And the counterfeiting spirit becometh the receiver of the soul, being assigned unto it and transferring it according to the chastisement because of the sins which it hath made it commit, and is in great enmity to the soul.

And when the soul hath finished the chastisements in the chaos according to the sins, which it hath committed, the counterfeiting spirit leadeth it forth out of the chaos, being assigned unto it and transferring it to every region because of the sins which it hath committed; and it leadeth it forth on the way of the rulers of the midst. And when it reacheth them, the rulers question it on the mysteries of the destiny; and if it hath not found them, they question their destiny. And those rulers chastise that soul according to the sins of which it is guilty. I will tell you the type of their chastisements at the expansion of the universe. When therefore, the time of the chastisements of that soul in the judgements of the rulers of the midst shall completed, the counterfeiting spirit leadeth the soul up out of all the regions of the rulers of the midst and bringeth it before the light of the sun according to the commandment of the First Man, Yew, and bringeth it before the judge, the virgin of Light. And she proveth that soul and findeth that it is a sinning soul, and casteth her light-power into it for its standing-upright and because of the body and the community of sense, the type of which I will tell you at the expansion of the universe. And the Virgin of Light sealeth that soul and handeth it over to one of her receivers and will have it cast into a body which is suitable to the sins which it hath committed. And amen, I said unto you: they will not discharge that soul from the changes of the body until it hath yielded its last circuit according to its merit. Of all these then will I tell you their type and the type of the bodies into which it will be cast according to the sins of each soul. All this will I tell you when I shall have told you the expansion of the universe."

(Third book chapter 111:284-286, Pistis Sophia A Gnostic Gospel G.R.S. Mead ed. 1984).

I started to think about our mission on this planet. Was it to strengthen our soul through tests and by the clearing of our karma (past life and present sins) to become pure in the eyes of our Eternal Father? By finding and following and fulfilling our missions, we will become brighter souls. Our higher vibrations would purify the impure and enable us to reunite ourselves with the Whole. Once our goal has been achieved we shall be

"Finally, be strong in the Lord and in his mighty power. Put on the full armour of God so that you can take your stand against the devil's schemes. For our struggle is not against flesh and blood, but against the rulers (archons), against the authorities, against the powers of this dark world and against the spiritual forces of evil in the heavily realms. Therefore put on the full armour of God, so that when the day of evil comes, you may be able to stand your ground, and after you have done everything, to stand. Stand firm then, with the belt of truth buckled round your waist, with the breastplate of righteousness in place, and with your feet fitted with readiness that comes from the gospel of peace. In addition to all this, take up the shield of faith, which you can extinguish all the flaming arrows of the evil one. Take the helmet of salvation and sword of the spirit, which is the word of God. And pray in Spirit, in all occasions with all kinds of prayers and request. With this in mind, be alert and always keep on praying for all the Saints." Ephesians 6:10-18 Holy Bible.*

ready to convert the energies and ensure Divine Love and Light prevail, so guaranteeing the birth and continuing growth of new star systems therefore permitting the expansion of all of the Universes.

"Whoever has something in hand will be given more, and whoever has nothing will be deprived of even the little that person has."
Saying 41 – Nag Hammadi Scriptures Gospel of Thomas by Marvin Meyer (2007).

Through these visions and dreams it was revealed and confirmed to me that we are living in multi-dimensions realities. This is again explained in the *Law of Correspondence – As Above As Below – Universal Laws*, meaning that how we direct our thoughts, emotions, words, and actions has an impact on the battle between Light and darkness being waged for the future of our race.

One night, while I was in bed my connection was strong and the pressure on my forehead was intense, I felt that my body was trying to hover in the air and that I was being lifted from my bed. My hands started to move slowly with grace of their own accord starting to feed my chakras with Light I was collecting from above and found myself surrounded by beautiful energies.

This was my first experience of my hands movements being guided by higher force but, since then, this has happened every time I meditate or attune with higher energies for any purpose. I always could control them if I wanted, but it is right to leave them moving around with movements so graceful, gentle, and beautiful to watch.

I questioned my Masters and Guides about this development, but only received my answer after a year of further study.

It is the Helper, The Shekinah, The Divine Presence, The Holy Spirit, which comes within us when our vibration is high enough to set off on our soul/journeys to other dimensions. The negative influences within our Third dimension make this merger impossible to occur within us, as it is only through the raising of our vibrations by applying the Law of Vibration – Universal Law (the monitoring of our thoughts, emotions, words and actions, and by transmuting them from negative to positive or higher principles) are we able to journey and can we experience this Inner Divine

Presence. It is a creative force and once this Presence is within us, we need to be cautious and responsible with our actions in order to not risk imprisoning it within the inner reality of our ego. We need to live in Truth and Peace in order to nurture Her power, to let Her start to stimulate us for the call out when it is ready for the merging with Grace and Righteousness!

During my holiday I also started to experience an increase in intensity of the pain still lying in my left shoulder, which had been with me for months now. After trying to heal it myself, and finding only temporary relief, I understood it was best to leave it alone. When the time is right it would go away on its own in the same way it had come.

After so many events, and for the next few months, I found that I wanted to share my experiences with other people around me to get a variety of some opinions, but I quickly discovered that I was on my own and I ended up more isolated, before I understood it was the way needed to be.

"Blessings on those who are alone and chosen, for you will find the kingdom. For you have come from it, and you will return there again."
Saying 49 – Nag Hammadi Scriptures Gospel of Thomas by Marvin Meyer (2007).

To the few who were more receptive, I gave what I knew. So, in fact, I did manage to begin to put words and actions to what I had been receiving, while still dealing with my own challenge of controlling my thoughts, emotions, words and actions in real life situations - not always easy!

"Jesus Said, A prophet is not acceptable in the prophet's own town; a doctor does not heal those who know the doctor."
Saying 31 – Nag Hammadi Scriptures Gospel of Thomas by Marvin Meyer (2007).

I was trying my best to learn and understand that this real life situation is all part of a big illusion, an illusion that I could make part of my life again if I would behave as I always used to behave, acting as the victim or the perpetuator, feeding my ego and losing myself in this time and space, forgetting and leaving behind my development of the past year.

Nearing the end of my stay in Tanzania, I was sitting at the back of a small 12 passenger aeroplane when we were hit by a violent windshear on our final approach for landing. As I was eating a boiled egg the plane lurched violently, my egg was hurled forward and went to meet the pilot on the front. Luckily the skill of the pilot meant that the plane did not crash, and my boiled egg was returned to me intact. After this near crash I started to have other strong visions. This time I saw the animals spirits, large African elephants with huge tusks, huge grotesque dinosaurs shrouded in a fusion of many different colours and violent storm of light, signifying to me that there was another battle going on. Then I saw eyes, some faces of very grotesque figures, and I was being guided to send golden light and love to them. Within me there was a strong aim to convert this light with the power of Love, bring it into God's Will and let him restore and recycle it again. *Everything comes from the Creator and to the Creator they must return.* While I was doing this with my eyes closed, the plane was in a very turbulent state and everyone was dead silent, but I was feeling fearless and invincible. This vision lasted for hours and I saw the beauty and the holiness of the Holy Spirit, again with a bluish and other coloured flames, and I was happy and grateful, paying my respects and giving my thanks by saying, 'Holy, Holy, Holy God Is Glory.' The same night, again I saw the same figure of the warrior, whom I had seen at the beginning of my trip and He was delivering me other gifts.

While I was at camp and during my game drives, I used to have strong downloads where I was being guided to visualise the Golden Light in my surrounding and emanate it from my heart chakra, I was also instructed to open a sacred place within the camp in this beautiful place, which I did.
On my return to home, I did not feel very well. I went to work the next day, but I decided to return home early and go to bed. While I was in bed I was with the Light and my hands were again being guided moving around, as if they where healing my body. There was a fair amount of energy channelling through me and the pain in my shoulder, although still there was less. As my hands were moving I could sense the presence of a magnetic field around them with great energy out of them - more than I had experience before.

Chapter 20

Finding the Light

On my return from Africa, I was living in a state of confusion, unable to decipher any of the events occurring around me. This frustrated me both in and out, in my meditations I felt some blockages and the worse one was my heart chakra, the energies were not flowing properly because of these blockages the energies coming from above they were stopping in my heart chakra giving me an intense discomforts with a sensation of being crashed by an enormous pressure. It was again a big knot in my heart. It was as though somebody had put a big rock on it. This feeling persisted for a few days, and I did not know what to do. My inner guidance was advice me no to fight it, to have faith and continuing to keep an open mind, by applying lovely thoughts, loving manners, and kind actions and this problem should clear up. I felt, I was going through another spiritual transformation. Eventually, I understood why all this was occurring. It was revealed to me in one of my mediations. This is what have happened.

When I used to do my "soul/journey meditation", which was my aim, as I previously mentioned, to go to other worlds or dimensions, I was journeying when it was requested by my Guides, usually a couple of times a week. But lately, because my blockages it had been more than three weeks now since my last journeying. Once again I was been asked to journey again, but after such a long break I felt that I couldn't manage it. Normally, I would journey by first trying to relax and slow down all my mental activity by listening a relaxing music and using the technic of the seven breaths I was attuning with the music and visualising myself going through the Tree of Life and going upwards, past all the other dimensions or kingdoms until I reached the 5th dimension or kingdom, there I would meet the gatekeeper of the 5th Kingdom and ask permission to enter, after meeting my Spiritual Parents (very bright Light) I was being led to my Original Self or Higher Self (another bright Light), where I would merge with Him and together journey to other kingdoms and places out there in the universe. It was only through the merging of my Higher Self that I could journey, because He holds the keys of the *Merkabah* the vehicle of ascension. When merged with my Higher Self I never knew what the outcome was, and the beauty of all this was to leave my mind free to travel through space with no time. It was always different and an amazing experience.

But now, I was guided in a different way. I started by looking for the Light and when I was finding the Light, I stayed with it. At first it was very hard for me to see the Light, also because everytime I was doing it I was been disturbed by persistant external noises, in fact, it took me a long time before I could connect with the Light, but then once I saw the Light I was guided to stay and contemplate the Light. I didn't need anymore to go up through the Tree of Life, to the 5th kingdom and merge with my Higher Self. I was told that from this meditation on, I needed to trust more my inner voice, and hear it, as the daily guidance.

"Look to the Living one as long as you live, or you might die and then try to see the Living one, and you will not be able to see."
Saying 59 – Nag Hammadi Scriptures Gospel of Thomas by Marvin Meyer
(2007).

I remember the discomfort I suffered during these days from these blockages, but I was guided to do the same meditation again and again, staying with the Light, and I could see and feel how staying with the Light I was absorbing the Light, and the Light was removing these blockages but the next day I was dealing with them once again.

For the next three days I was guided to find the Light, trying to remove this blockages and once the energies within were flowing freely, I was been told to visualise two pyramids one in front of me, with its base positioned on my chest and their apex looking outwards, and one on my back with its base facing the one of the front. I was trying to make them spin one clockwise and the other anticlockwise, with their based connected, it was easy at low speed, but when I was increasing their speed they were wobbling, and everytime I was doing this, I was been constantly disturbed by phone ringing, dogs barking etc. I could not manage to reach the point were my Guide was leading me!

The second day while I was doing this process staying with the Light and letting the energies to flow below my heart chakra, something unusual happened, when I just managed to remove the blockage of my heart chakra, a beautiful *story of Joseph, son of Jacob, from the Holy Bible Genesis 37-50* came into my mind.

I read this story once, and it was like I knew it very well, I remembered the hatred and the jealousy of the older brothers towards Joseph, being the favourite son of Jacob. I saw when the brothers sold him as a slave and serving in a house of a rich person in Egypt, when he ended up in prison in Egypt and when because of his gift to interpret dreams, he became the second most powerful man in Egypt. And I remember that I was going through his emotional feeling of how he missed his little brother Benjamin and his father Jacob and the fact he had no hatred towards the older brothers. He was ready to forgive them and in the end they were all reunited. And I was experiencing all the emotions of his situation feeling very overwhelmed. It was beautiful!

After this visions, I tried with the rotation of the pyramids, as I did yesterday, but again I could not succeed to make them spin faster, for the same reason mentioned previously!

It was the third day, I was repeating the same meditation and I still had blockages, my hands were moving on their own making symbols and placing them in some of the chakras and then feeding my chakras. I really did not have a clue what was going on during these meditations; but now something peculiar happened. By proceeding with the same meditation, finding and staying with the Light, opening my heart chakra and visualising two pyramids spinning in their opposite direction, one in front and one behind my chest,

Like the past two days. This time I focused all my attention on them, asking also the help of my Master and Angels, and when I started to increase their spin I was trying to keep them balance and when they were wobbling I was adjusting the speed a bit, until they were in a constant speed. Then I increased their speed commanding them to reach a speed of light and at the same time a point of stillness, once they were in balance and at full speed, I saw several more pyramids came from all directions to connect with the original two, and once this was accomplished, it was like the creation of a fusion of an atomic reaction, and massive bright Light appeared. It was like a star was born and I saw an expansive brightness, and while this was happening I saw my Master coming into me. I was amazed and surprised by these happenings! Afterwards, I don't know how long it lasted; my hands were feeding my chakras. The one I felt the most was the base chakra, in which I could feel the energies going upstream to the crown. So my heart blockage was being unblocked.

"Images are visible to people, but the light within them is hidden in the image of the father's Light. He will be disclosed, but his image is hidden by his Light."
Saying 83 – Nag Hammadi Scriptures Gospel of Thomas by Marvin Meyer
(2007).

That same night, I heard distorted voices with very hard accents and what sounded like an old dialect, it was Aramaic and energies vibrating around my head woke me up and I saw a lot of movement of energies in the room.

The *Merkabah* can manifest itself in many form the most common is the two Tetrahedrons merge together with their apexes looking in the opposite direction and forming the *Star of David*, the halves rotate in the opposite directions this allow the movement, but at the beginning of my journeys I was not seeing the *Merkabah*, I was only merging with the Light of my Higher Self, but after this experience I did not need anymore to go to the Upper World and through the Tree Of Life meditation to merge with my Higher Self in order I could journey to other realities, He was in me within the Light I needed only to attune and stay with the Light!

Shortly after this experience I was leaving for a diving holiday in the Red

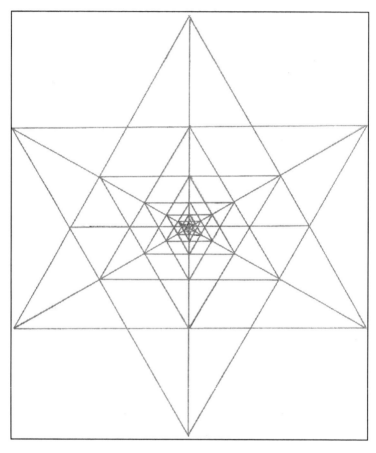

Merkabah is the interconnection between higher intellingence operating within myri-
ads of universes with their respective earth systems of life intellingence on a parallel
phase. We are one singularity of light within the pluralism of the Divine Light.
The Book of Knowledge: The Keys of Enoch, Key 301:20 by Dr J J Hurtak

Sea with my partner on a live-aboard boat. We were going to meet my friend Angelo in London, who was flying from Italy to join us on this holiday. The boat was departing from Marsa Alam, Egypt, to sail into Port Sudan. That night in London I felt very strange. Some visions I saw with my inner eye included lots of ancient symbols and letters scrolling into my mind very fast. I believe they were a mix of Egyptian, Aramaic, Hebrew and Greek letters.

On 31st October we embarked on the boat that was going to sail that same night, but this trip resulted in tragedy, a diver got lost inside a wreck. I was been asked by the instructors of the boat to help with their search for the lost diver, and at that time also I was consulting my guides to know where to search, but I could not get clear answers. During my staying on the boat I could not meditate, it was very difficult for me. I felt my connection was weak and the colours I normally see as brightly were very cloudy and faded, not at all clear. I felt deceived. My partner and I and some of the people on the boat, really did our best to help find this diver.

The diver was eventually found a few days later. He was still inside a wreck in the anchor chamber, without his air, weight belt and mask. We felt very sorry that we could not save his life.

On this trip it was one problem after another. It started at the very outset of the trip, when my partner and I nearly left the boat to return to Britain because my partner's grandmother was very ill She died shortly after we came back from our holiday. Then there was water contamination on the boat, which left a few of us with upset stomachs and diarrhoea. So, all in all, it was not a very successful trip.

On 12th November we returned to the UK and when I was in the car close to home I could feel my aura expand again, and the sensation of heaviness was gone. I could feel and see the Light again!

Chapter 21

Keeping on Searching

I was devouring books one after the other, driven by a compulsion to extend my knowledge through books that I was guided to meaning. I was reading particular books at specific times, in a defined sequence that helped me to absorb the meanings of the content quicker.

It was at this time that I understood – a true Master never gives his student the answers; rather they lead the student to discover them through self-realisation, thus mastering the knowledge by himself. They guide the student to it, through stimulation, but never spoil the pleasure of letting him uncover his own answers. Therefore I tried to be open-minded taking in as much information as possible and I used to get very excited whenever I was reading a new book, because I never knew what to expect and what was going to be unveiled to me.

I read books about the mysteries of the Qabalah – The Tree of Life, The Ten Sephiroth with their 32 Paths, the secrets of Gematria, Temurah and Notariquon, amongst others. During these readings I was been stimulated to conduct on further research and changes I needed to make to continue on with my spiritual journey. Some of these important decisions were the planning of my spiritual trips to Machu Picchu, Peru` in April 2010 and Uluru Rock (Ayers), Australia in November 2010. Another critical development was the integration of sacred names and expressions into my meditation by using a book called. '*The Seventy Two Living Divine Names of*

The Most High' By Dr J J Hurtak.

Meditating with the sacred names was different, and this book include 72 Sacred Living Names of The Most High chosen by Dr. J J Hurtak, and written in Aramaic, Hebrew and Greek. My understanding regarding these Names, together with many other Names of God known to us, were in the bible, but they had been removed a few centuries ago because they were considered to be too sacred to be pronounced, or for other reasons.

Quickly I realised the power of the Names, which are the Essence of the Living God. Each one of them retains the original vibration of God given to our prophets and seers on Earth. The Names describe what God really is.

The essence of God can be found in any sacred names given to humanity in the course of our human existence for the purpose of our evolution. I used the sacred names and expressions to raise my vibration, as keys to unlocking threshold gates, when praying by absorbing their essences and activating the Pillar of Light, which in turn helped me to be with the Light, I found I was singing them into the Light. Although I didn't understand why. Later I comprehended it was to purify the light into the Light, the Fire that eats the fire.

One by one, without realising I learnt all the Seventy Two Names - each day, a different Sacred Name and different vibration and different experience. For me, every day in my meditation was like witnessing a new miracle. The power and intensity of the Names was sometimes more, sometimes less, but never the same.

I also had a few dreams which emphasised the fact that most of us we do not have control of our own destiny. Once we discover the God within, we gain control of our future. Yet again, I could not grasp the reason for this until later in my journey exactly a year later, after reading another book called Pistis Sophia on my return from Australia.

"Let those who love the Lord hate evil,
For he guards the lives of his faithful ones
And delivers them from the hand of the wicked.
Light is shed upon the righteous

And joy on the upright in
Heart.
Rejoice in the Lord, you who are righteous,
And praise his Holy Name."
Psalms 97:10-12 Holy Bible

Next I read: *'We, The Arthurians'* by Norma Milanovich, with Betty Rice and Cynthia Ploski (1994). In this book Dr. Milanovich channels the Arthurians and provided me many more welcome truths and answers. I was excited and intrigued by all the information I gained, but one thing that shocked me was a sketch of a typical Arthurian face channelled by Dr. Milanovich using a crystal cluster, and that face was the same as those I had seen nearly a year ago during my awakening. I saw them next to me, and I saw them more than once. The Arthurians were short in height, and wearing Darth Vader type masks, like in the Star Wars film. When I saw the drawing it clarified matters for me. By then, I was well into the book and, more than anything, I knew I was on the right path!

I re-read some parts of the Bible over the Christmas period while I was away at my brother's house, and from there I got my healing stones which I called *'Heaven on Earth' stones*, and I now use in every meditation surrounding my sacred space. Another beautiful book that I read was: *'The Aquarian Gospel of Jesus The Christ'* by Levi, a book written over one hundred years ago. Levi, through his meditation, tapped into the Universal Mind (Holy Spirit) which revealed all to him about the life of Christ Jesus and His ministry until the ascension. This book includes the missing years, when Jesus travelled to other countries, and His passing of the test of initiation and His wisdom before the last three years, which is known to all of us.

All these books served to confirm my way, gave me access to new answers that were buried within me and also revealed some new truths. Together they helped me progress further along my path to the Light.

At this time I had some warning dreams. So I was guided to start to attune with crystals and keep them with me or around me, especially quartz and amethyst, to create more protection. I was determined to find ways to get clear message from above without being deceived by other forces. Sometimes, in my meditations I was seeing grotesque figures and I felt under attack in several instances, and I now believe there are months of the year when there are more negative influences than at other times, which has to do with the alignment of the constellations, stars, planets, sun and moon with Earth. The aim of these forces was a concentrated effort to stop me using the fear, and taking away the Light I was acquiring. I was not waiver but carried on regardless, defying them. This happened several time during my spiritual journey, but I always faced them with the help of my guides. I felt protected. Even at times of weakness, I managed to overcome them, with the help of my secret weapons - the knowledge of the sacred names that I had learnt.

One night, I was so awake and I was asking, what next? I wanted to go forwards and I felt strongly to carry on my studies and research looking for more knowledge in order I could reach the Gates of Wisdom. I called my guides, to see if I could get any tips or directions, then, I found myself in a vision:

I saw black tunnels and the connection on my forehead was getting very strong. I only remember some of the scenes. I saw some distorted faces; I did not know if they were good or bad, then Suns, then Pyramids, The Eye of Horus and then I saw Jesus and he showed me the way to go. I looked ahead and I saw on top of the pyramid an Angel in armour waiting for me. He took me through thresholds and tunnels of light and I saw many mountains. Finally, on top of one mountain there was a temple. The Angel dropped me there. I saw a big throne and a giant being. He took me in his hands, and I saw all etheric gifts given to me by the Holy Spirit months before.

Chapter 22

Following Guidance

As mentioned before, one of the ways I was getting my guidance was through the dowsing with a pendant although now I started to question the accuracy of the answers.

Since very ancient times, our ancestors used all sorts of tools to receive guidance from above: high priests used precious stones, sticks, animal bones, cards, letters, and many other implements to get in touch with the spirit world. But I felt things needed to change, because the answers recently received did not agree with the result of my daily reality. After this realisation I tried not to rely on dowsing any more. I got confirmation that our ego from within manipulated and deceived the answers. While this questioning of the reliability of the pendant was going on, one morning I got up and I found my pendant mysteriously broken. This was a sign for me not to use it again. I needed to listen with discernment and then trust my inner guidance - which some people call intuition. I was using this a lot during my meditation, but not in my daily life. Rapidly I learnt also to discern answers coming from the inner universe, because our ego or lower self can also whisper to us and deceive us. He masks himself as guide but, in reality, he is a deceiver, with a aim of creating confusion by lying to us and undermining our confidence. This is what happens when we are not living in harmony ourselves.

I was having meaningful dreams trying to deliver me guidance. Dreams always have a hidden meaning, and it is important no to confuse guidance with dreams that come from the astral plane. The purpose of astral plane dreams is to steal, and it is the place where most of the time our consciousness resides. I was attempting to analyse the meanings behind them but some of them I could not understand or make any sense of at the time. Later on I realised they were premonition depicting the future and it was because they had not happened yet that I couldn't comprehend them.

Changing the way I received my guidance helped me greatly; I believe it accelerated my progress along the path even more. I started to seeking my inner voice deep within and understood the real value of channelling to get higher guidance. We are made to receive whether we know it or not, we are made to channel energies and consciousness, most of the time without knowing it.

> *"All praising Him and saying, 'Holy, Holy, Holy,*
> *AAA, HHH, EEE, III, OOO, YYY, - That is to say,' Thou art the Living One of*
> *Living Ones, Holy of Holies, Beings of Beings, Father of Fathers, God of Gods,*
> *Lord of Lords, Space of Spaces' They praise Him saying 'Thou art the House and*
> *the Dweller in the House' they praise Him , saying unto the Son concealed in Him,*
> *'Thou art: Thou art, O Alone-begotten, Light and Life and Grace."*
> *Page. 36 The Gnosis of Light A Translation of the Untitled Apocalypse contained in*
> *the Brucianus Codex by F Lampugh and R.A. Gilbert (2006)*

I noticed when connecting with my Guides my right side of the brain used to get very hot, and it was around that time I read a book regarding channelling. This book - *Opening To Channel. How to Connect With Your Guide* by Sanaya Roman and Duane Parker (1987) - is beautifully written. It describes lots transmissions channelled by higher guides whom I used to feel their vibrations by reading their messages, and I knew they were coming from higher beings. This book increased my awareness of how high energies come into our bodies. It is written in a very simple way to help us understand and experience channelling energies.

"Jesus said, from Adam to John the Baptizer, among those born of women, there is

no one greater than John the Baptizer, so that his eyes should not be averted. But I have said that whoever among you becomes a child will know the kingdom and will become greater than John."

Saying 46 - Nag Hammadi Scriptures Gospel of Thomas by Marvin Meyer (2007).

Part Three

In this part of the book, I was meditating by chanting all the Names, I was seeing the Light I was with the Light, and contemplating the Light; visualization was not required anymore to reach the Light. I had other experiences too. I was applying more of my learning to my daily life. I felt it important to commit myself more into it.

I left my job and was then fully absorbed with my path. It was at that time when I began to re-write this book, which I completed within a year. I received other gifts in forms of new Names, but I did not have so many soul-journeys or strong visions like I had in the past year. This time was all about striving to find my answers, and discovering meanings. I started to piece all the parts of the puzzle together, based on my personal experiences. And, in additions of this, I came to fully understand the power of Prayer.

"Wisdom is acquired with Faith and with Seeking, and Discerning the Findings."

Chapter 23

Unveiling The Snake

Through my studies I was finding information and answers that were bothering me on a daily basis, the meaning of the snake was one of them, I wanted to understand: who is the snake really and what is it's role and meanings to humanity? This was one of the mysteries I needed to solve and during my research to my surprise, I discovered that the role of the snake in humanity was more than just a symbolic figure.

I realised that the snake is present in all ancient civilizations, a figure of hatred and fear in some and worshipped by others. It has been depicted as a perpetrator, a liberator, a healer and a deceiver. In fact, we will find the symbolic figure of the snake in many ancient cultures and civilizations. The Egyptians for example, show the snake in many of their monuments and hieroglyphics, where it emerges out from the third eye meaning the bringing of knowledge and power. In Tibetan culture it is known as the power of Kundalini, which symbolises transformation and enlightening - Lord Buddha was under the hood of a cobra when He became self-realised. In Sanskrit, the main representation of the snake is given by the Deity God Shiva shown a cobra always around his/her neck, symbolising the conquering of a deadly power of destruction and the renewal of the connection with cosmic forces. The "Feathered Snake with wings" was the representation of Quetzalcoatl one of the main deity for the Aztecs, Toltecs, Mayan and other Middle American peoples, for whom He was the creator sky-god and wise legislator. The snake is in the myth of Ida and Pingala – the two snakes entwined –

symbolising balance between male and female. The ancient Greeks had the caduceus (herald's wand) of the god Hermes, intertwined snakes with two wings on top, representing a balanced, supreme rulership an image which we in the western still use as a logo for medical healing. The most symbolic figure of the snake in the western cultures is in the biblical story of Adam and Eve. Here the snake is the deceiver and tempter who led Eve to convince Adam to eat from the Tree of the Knowledge of Good and Evil. In order words, according to the ancient scriptures, the snake brought duality into our consciousness; not only in the depiction of both good and evil but also in the underlying power of sensuality. For the natives of the Americas it represents transformation and transmutation - it coils itself around releasing our past in the same way it sheds his own skin - *it has the power of creation, for it embodies sexuality, psychic energy, alchemy, reproduction and Ascension (or immortality) - Medicine Card by* Jamie Sams & David Carson.

In Aboriginal culture there are two snakes for them: the rainbow snake is the creator of all, and the black snake is the poisonous one signifying destruction. The Aboriginals also tell us a story of a war between the two snakes, good and evil one to the south of Uluru Rock and one to the north, representing the Divine and the ego, which could well be replicated by the two sides of our brain, right and left.

If we do a more intense research on the traditional or symbolic/spiritual meaning of the snake we will find it everywhere on this planet. In any tradition around the world the snake is given a meaning or a role of one kind or the another, good or evil and definitely has an imprint on each one of us.

So, what is it the reality of the snake? Is it good or bad? Why do people always give spiritual meaning to the snake?

In my personal experience, I saw the spirit of the snake, and it was a cobra. It awakened me one night, living both within and without and when, after several times I demanded it show itself so I could understand who was masked behind these massive energies, finally revealed itself and appeared to me. It reared up in front of me and bared its fangs in an attempt to scare me, but I was only surprised at that time.

During my studies I found this beautiful and powerful description of the snake from a book full of wisdom. Which I copied as a reference:

Qabalistic Definition of the Snake Nachash (שׁנ)

The word according to the secret tradition designates the deep interior feeling binding an entity to its own individual existence, making it ardently desire to preserve and enlarge it.

Nachash, the snake within a man is the radical egoism which causes an individual being to make of itself a center and to relate everything else to it. Moses defines this sentiment as seducing passion of elementary nature and the secret spring with which the Creator has provided all (animate) things in nature; we know it by the name of nature instinct. Nachash is not to be understood as separate being, but rather as central movement given to matter, a hidden spring acting in the depths of things. The self-seeking elements within a man, the blind passions common to us all in our early stages of evolution are the offspring's of this snake Nachash. This word stand for unreasoning self –center instinct in all the oriental languages, it means an internal ardour, a centralized fire, agitated by a violent movement and seeking to extend itself. The Chaldaic derives from it all ideas of fears, sorrow, anxiety and evil, and painful passions. In Arabic, Syriac and Ethiopian it signifies a tormenting affliction.

And it goes again:

Lesson of the Nachash (Snake)

All love emotions are expansive, all emotions of hatred are restrictive. Hope and faith are the nature of love and expand the soul, while fear, doubt and despair is the nature of hate and contract the souls, making feel uneasy, and unhappy. The snake stands for contraction, for tightness and in drawings; while men fight and quarrel with one another they always resemble more or less the old snake, each drawing to its side, anxious for self-preservation. Freedom from the snake's anguish can only be had by ceasing from the snake's ways, and learning to obey the law of love, the first dictate of which is self-sacrifice.

The Mystery of the Qabalah the Yogi Publication written by seven pupils of E. G. Page. 14-15.

"Since the children have flesh and blood, he too shared in their humanity so that by his death he might destroy him who holds the power of death – that is, the devil –

and free those who all their lives were held in slavery by their fear of death."
Hebrew 2:14-15 Holy Bible.

The snake is not only ego, but also is a symbol of Death and, together with Lion-face (which is a form of shining light), is a destructive light power encoded in the limited light and we as humans are entrapped within it!

"And Self-Willed (Authades) sent out of the height, from the thirteenth aeon, another great light-power. Like a flying arrow it entered the chaos to help his emanations, so that they might seize once more the lights of Pistis Sophia of the thirteenth aeon. And when that light-power had entered the chaos, the emanations of Self-Willed which were oppressing Pistis Sophia were greatly encouraged, and with terrors and harassment they again pursued her. And some emanations of the Self-Willed then began to press upon her. One of them transformed itself into a shape of a great serpent; another the shape of a seven-headed basilisk; another into the shape of a dragon. And the first power of the Self-Willed, the one with Lion-face and all his many other emanations, united to besiege Pistis Sophia together, and they dragged her back into the lower regions of chaos and began to torment her. Page 318,319,320 Book 2 Chapter 66:136 Pistis Sophia A Coptic Text Of Gnosis With Commentary by PhD J J and Desiree Hurtak.

These are the emanations of the rulers who have ruled our world even before Adam and Eve and they have been acknowledged after eating from the tree of knowledge of good and evil!

When I knew of the presence of these realities, I understood who the enemies were, and how to fight them. I was called into the battleground, into the fight and I started down the path of the spiritual warrior, fighting for the Light.

"He who dwells in the shelter of the
Most High El El Elyon
will rest in the shadow of the
Almighty. El Shaddhai

I will say of the Lord Adonai,' He is my refuge and my fortress, Elohim Misgabi
my God Yahweh,
in whom I trust
surely he will save you from the fowler's snare
and from the deadly pestilence,
he will cover you with his feathers,
and under his wings you will find
refuge;
His faithfulness will be your shield
and rampart.
You will not fear the terror of night,
nor the arrow that flies by day,
nor the pestilence that stalks in the
darkness,
nor the plague that destroys at
midday.
a thousand may fall at your side,
ten thousand at your right hand,
but it will not come near you.
You will only observe with your eyes
and see the punishment of the
wicked.
If you make the Most High El El Elyon your
dwelling -
even the Lord Adonai,
Who is my refuge Elohim Misgabi.
Then no harm will befall you,
no disaster will come near your
tent.
For he will command his angels
concerning you
to guard you in all your ways;
they will lift you up in their hands,

so that you will not strike your foot
against a stone.
You will tread upon the lion and the
cobra;
you will trample the great lion and
the serpent.
Because he loves me, says the Lord Adonai,
I will rescue him;
I will protect him, for he
acknowledges my Name.
He will call upon me, and I will answer
Him;
I will be with him in trouble,
I will deliver him and honour him.
with long life will I satisfy him
and show him my salvation."
Psalm 91 Holy Bible

Since then, the snake has brought to my attention all my fears, all my unfinished business, all past records to deal with. He has tempted me, tried to scare me, tried to confuse me, tried to seed war within and without and, at times, because of my ignorance, he has deceived me!

Then during my journey, I understood the way! It starts through Faith and Repentance (Hope) but they alone are not enough; it requires knowledge to understand and that is why I was being guided to read and study ever deeper. But also when Faith reaches Wisdom, they still need Love, the transforming power!

If the snake is our ego, the lion face is represented by our sun and is a self-combusting light, which is consumes itself until extinction! They will try their best to make us believe that we are an island - an individual and they will try their best to make us live according to our senses and desires, convincing us that there is no other reality besides the reality which is dictated by our five senses which they claim is heaven. They make us believe that we are in charge of ourselves and there is no manipulation and things happen because of coincidences or because of nature. They make us believe that God is a figure to share with individuals in order to give a simplistic reason for our existence. These powers make us believe that man is the god on earth and that our matter (brain) is in charge, but, from the point of the higher truths, these powers are present because they need to be transmuted much like the Hindi Deity Shiva, who has conquered death and wears the cobra around the neck. Once the snake and the lion face have been conquered we are ready for the transformation. This is also what the Egyptian Sphinx wants to tell us, a body of a lion representing our solar system, and the face of a human. By overcoming these forces, our birthright it is regained together with all the things that have been stolen from us and shall be returned to us. In one level of truths, these forces have made us live in darkness so we could not reach the Higher Kingdom of Light and regain the Trees of our rewards. This is the reason why many Lords like Buddha and Jesus have descended to rescue us. We need to shed our skin, in order that Our Saviour can bring enlightenment to us!

"Blessed is the lion that the human will eat, so that lion becomes human. And cursed is the human that the lion will eat, and the lion became human."
Saying 7 – Nag Hammadi Scriptures Gospel of Thomas by Marvin Meyer
(2007).

And then the serpent became Kundalini - The Serpent of Light, Ida and Pingala became one, creating balance and peace and Quetzalcoatl will wear His Feathered Garment of Light with its wings for his Ascension.

"To transform these powers, God gave us the Names, Humility Faith and Will to pursue Wisdom, and with Love these are our weapon."

"And the first will be the last and the last the first."

These powers and spirits are real, powerful and capable of manipulated our life for their benefit.

"Whoever does not hate father and mother cannot be a follower of me, and whoever does not hate brothers and sisters and bear the cross as I do will not be worthy of me."
Saying 55 – Nag Hammadi Scriptures Gospel of Thomas by Marvin Meyer (2007).

This is what I know about the Cobra and other powers, which I shared with you, those who already know them and those who don't.

Chapter 24

Grace and The New Sacred Names of the Most High

It was a month before my trip to Peru` and I had been meditating every day with the Sacred Names of the Most High. Since starting this new way of meditation a few months earlier, I chanted the Names the best I could until I was guided to the right Name for my daily meditation. Then, I was focusing on the Light and repeating the chosen Name seven times.

During these meditations, I was dealing with my inner universe, and I was experiencing strong energies coming from above through my crown chakra and into my physical body, raising the Light within. In the meantime I was still feeding my chakras with my hands as I used to do, this time with the Light created by the vibration of the Name.

This Light was travelling within through my spine. It was like a river flowing down and clearing any impediment along it's route and the Light within was getting stronger and stronger; I no longer needed the aid of visualisation technique as, by now, I could see the Light. I was doing this meditation every day with a different Name and the aim was to attune only with Light, without looking at anything else, just contemplating only the Light in front of me. The more I stayed with the Light chanting the Names, the more my whole body was adsorbing the Light. My entire face was being illuminated and from time to time also all of my body. One day during my meditation after I chanted the Name, I saw and felt a gentle expansive Light, different to the other light. It was so bright and beautiful; this Light brought me warmth to the outside of my body as well the inside, it was like a veil of silk that was embracing all my body in and out. I felt loved! Time became irrelevant and I was in a state of absolute stillness; the Light was bringing harmony, peace, beauty and love within and around me and later I realised this was Grace. After this episode, Grace was coming and visiting me from time to time during my meditation and when Grace was with me I was in stillness and time was always irrelevant. I could stay forever; it was Harmony and Beauty, Peace and Love together bringing divine warmth of belonging.

Quickly I had worked my way through all the 72 Sacred Names of my meditation book. Occasionally I was meditating with a Name I had meditated with in the past, but after a couple of months I reached the point where I knew all seventy-two Sacred Names and had absorbed their meaning and their full essences. I no longer needed to refer to the meditation book, for they were now all firmly imprinted in my consciousess! allowing me to be more focused on all the power of the Names and chanting them into the light.

One day, when I had chanted all 72 Names and had reached the last one, I was waiting for the guidance to tell me which Name to choose from the 72 listed Names of the book to meditate on, but to my surprise something different happened. While I was waiting for my answer, the Light was getting stronger and I was seeing Fire, very bright! And from the Fire I saw letters coming out and the letters were on fire. From that day and over the next couple of months, I was reaching the same status or place and I was receiving new Names! Some of these were a mix of the Seventy Two Divine Names of The Most High by Dr. Hurtak, and some were completely new.

"Whoever is near me is near the fire, and whoever is far from me is far from the kingdom."
Saying 82 – Nag Hammadi Scriptures Gospel of Thomas by Marvin Meyer (2007).

I didn't know what to believe, I was searching in books and on the Internet for the meaning of these Names but I did not find any plausible answers. The only thing I knew was that these Names were very powerful to me; through them I crossed new thresholds of light. The energies emanated by these Names were so strong that I sometimes found myself locked in my lotus position in pain, unable to move due to the huge amount of energy that I had channelled into my essence. I used these New Names to reach worlds where the Light was not present, I went to places where aliens life was present, but I never felt intimidated or in fear of harm from these life forms and, when I was in the midst of the darkness of these worlds, I was being told to chant the New Sacred Name aloud several times and anchor the emanated Light from Name into these places. I followed the instruction and witnessed this was what I did and that world which was darkness would become Light, like a star transformed from a tumultuous and dark environment to a calm, stable and brighten environment. When this was accomplished I was guided to leave and return to my domain.

After learning all 72 Sacred Names and receiving the New Names I started experiencing clicks and cracks within my brain - during my meditation sessions. They occurred in hundred's, sometimes reaching over a thousand every one gave me a sense of release - and I observed that the left part of my brain was creating resistance. I began to hear different types of sounds, varying day by day; there was a kind of humming sound, a high-pitched yet reassuring sound when I was attuned with the Light, a singing bowl sound and several others. Singing the Names opened up parts of my brain that connect directly with our Divine Father/Mother.

Hymn to the Creator

The Lord is great and holy, the Most Holy for generation after generation.
Majesty goes before him, and after him abundance of many waters.
Loving-kindness and truth are about his face; truth and judgement and righteousness are the pedestal of his throne.
He divides light from obscurity; he establishes the dawn by the knowledge of his heart.
When all his angels saw it, they sang, for they showed them that which they had not known.
He crowns the mountains with fruit, with good food for the living.
Blessed be the master of the earth with his power, who establishes the world by his wisdom.
By his understanding he stretched out the heaven, and brought forth wind from his stores.
He made lightning for the rain, and raised mist from the end of the earth.

Vermes, G., The Complete Dead Sea Scrolls in English Revised Edition, Penguin Books, London, 2004, Page 312-313. Prayer of Dead Sea Scroll Hymns and Poems.

Chapter 25

Peru - A Spiritual Trip

My trip to Peru was getting close and I still did not have a clear idea what I needed to do. My main aim was to visit Machu Picchu and as I was spending three days there to give me enough time to achieve what I needed to do.

A couple weeks before my trip, I remember watching the news and they were broadcasting that Machu Picchu was still closed after the floods problems in January. The Urubamba River flooded the sacred valley, destroying some of the houses, part of the roads and railway lines connected with Arguas Calientes - the village linked with Machu Picchu was completely cut off; in fact some tourists had to be flown out by helicopter. It was only a few days before my departure that they managed to repair some of the roads and railways. I thought that was a good sign!

"Do not worry, from morning to evening and from evening to morning, about what you will wear"
Saying 36 – Nag Hammadi Scriptures Gospel of Thomas by Marvin Meyer (2007).

The trip to Peru affected me from the beginning. First, while I was relaxing on the plane, I felt a massive download from my crown chakra, which lasted for hours and was the strongest I had recorded. It was like a part of my brain was going to collapse. I looked out of the window and I could see the islands of the Bahamas below and I remembered reading that here was one of the most powerful vortexes of energies on earth, encompassing the Bermuda Triangle, where the remains of the Atlantis lie submerged. This strong pressure lasted until I reach the Amazon Forest!

While I was flying above the Amazon forest I saw the beautiful deep green valleys carved by the muddy rivers and, before reaching Lima, I flew above the mountains that separated the forest from the Pacific ocean. I marvelled at the striking colour of the desert and the bare mountains with some patches of very light bright green. The sky was a very light clear blue. It was all so beautiful to see the contrast of so many of nature's colours together, a truly glorious scene. This is what I found in Peru; a mixing of bright colours.

I stayed in Lima for a night and then moved on to Cuzco, another unique place. I savoured the beauty of the majestic churches built by the Conquistadores on top of the Inca sacred site but I felt a sense of oppression at their desire to eradicate the beliefs of the indigenous people. I went inside the vanity of these cathedrals and within I found strong energies, coming from the stones or the ruins below. Through out the streets near the Temple of the Sun I was picking up vibrations as I explored the area visited other sacred places and all of them had been built with massive stones. These stones act as amplifiers to retain and increase vibrations enabling the old priest to connect with their spirits.

Finally, I was on the train to Machu Picchu where I met a Brazilian guy trying to practice his English language on me. He was into photography, constantly taking pictures of the surroundings and he told me without me forcing my views upon him that spirituality is our future disclosing that he was trying to learn how to meditate too.

Machu Picchu a phenomenal site. It is situated on top of Machu Picchu mountain - meaning ancient peak - and looks north toward Huayna Picchu - meaning young mountain. I was fortunate enough to be staying close by and went straight to the site as soon as I had dropped my bag at the hotel. It was early afternoon and while walking around the site I could feel energies everywhere most intensely around the Temple of the Condor (where the energies were shooting out from the cave), the Temple of the Moon and of course the Intihuatana stone.

I had read that people could climb the Huayna Picchu, although initially I was not sure about attempting it, due the dangers posed by the wet and slippery terrain, but my courage grew and I decided to tackle it the next day.

That morning I waited for the gate to open so that I could commence my climb of the peak I was surprised by the number of people assembled who shared my goal. The ascent would take about one hour and half – some of it passing through very steep ascents where one wrong step could result in a fall of several hundred metres. The climb was challenging and, though I was soon sweating, I soldiered on, pausing at one stage only to remove my sweater and I reached the summit before anyone else.

At the top I recited the Lord's Prayer and once other people arrived, I decided to descend. It was extremely foggy and the descent was as challenging as the ascent. I needed to be on time at the next place were I was being guided, therefore I came down the very narrow, steep and slippery paths quickly. On the way down I met many people attempting to reach the top - both young and old and some in sandals!

It was to the pyramid of Machu Picchu that I had been called by my guides. I sat on the east corner at the top and gazed at the Intihuatana Sacred Stone, relaxed while trying simultaneously to be attuned with the place. I stayed there for a couple of hours, but the only thing I saw or felt was a green flashing light and the general feeling of the energies around.

Throughout my stay at Machu Picchu I was meditating every day and the energies were strong but nothing out of ordinary happened which slightly disappointed me, so I walked to Argues Calientes and caught my train to the Sacred Valley, not knowing what to expect. I visited the town of Ollantaytambo and the Temple of the Sun and here the vibrations were incredibly strong. I wondered how and why the Incas had transported such large stones from hundreds of miles away. Even today with the use of our modern equipment to move such stones and place them on the top of a very steep mountain would be an almost impossible task,

People must ask themselves why these civilizations applied so much effort, time and energy and lost of so many lives, to build monuments like the Pyramids, Stonehenge, and Temples of the Sun, Machu Picchu, Chichen Itza, the Olympus Temple and many others around the world.

The reasons are so clear to me; these civilizations knew of the existence of God, together with other realities, and they knew under their spirit guidance how to contact the spirit world and indwell with them. They used particular stones, which were not always available in the local area and it did not matter to them if they needed to move these stones hundreds of miles taking years to complete their temples without regard for the human cost involved in such projects. These stones were very special for them, because they enabled these civilizations to connect and let these spirits to indwell with them, gathering insights and knowledge letting these spirits influence their lives. In fact, using their spiritual influences, ancient peoples built temples, cities and countries, which are still a mystery to us, some of the cities were built to mirror the Milky Way with such precision that even our scientists today struggle to find any explanations!

While in the Sacred Valley I met a guide who used to work with some leaders and groups of people from various spiritual organizations, (mainly from the US) and guided the groups to visit shamans for the purpose of receiving their blessing. He confided in me that, when he took these people to receive their blessings in Quechua language by the shamans (which of course the visitors could not understand) he was confused and horrified on hearing that the words being uttered by the shamans were indeed anything but blessings - rather they were comments of a very low nature! He told me these pilgrims had spent considerable amount of money to be here and they really believed there were receiving blessings. He felt ashamed of how these shamans were behaving. Until this time he viewed them as wise men with integrity, but this behaviour had changed his opinion of some of them.

"If a blind person leads a blind person, both of them will fall into a hole."
Saying 34 – Nag Hammadi Scriptures Gospel of Thomas by Marvin Meyer
(2007).

I believe this is the time, more than ever one must use discernment in order to avoid being deceived!

I want to conclude this account of my experience of Peru by mentioning the corruption and imbalances of these civilizations which brought them to kill even their brothers and sisters, as well as animals, in sacrifice to their gods. These priests, in all parts of the world, believed by sacrificing the blood of innocents they could redeem their own sins, their gods had got a hold of them and through manipulation and deception casting them into heavier chains and bringing more abominations on their heads! I believe it was this that brought about their own destruction.

"Day after day every priest stands and performs his religious duties; again and again he offers the same sacrifices, which can never take away the sins."
Hebrew 10:11 Holy Bible

Also, these atrocities were committed by fallen intelligence into some sacred land or place on Earth in order to be deconsecrated by bringing transgressions and violence in them trying to alienate the receptive part of our conciousness to stop the visitation and the influences of the Brotherhood of Light, some of these places were and some continuing to be, places were the high intelligence come and indwell with humans, guiding us to follow the right path! Places like the Middle East, Egypt, Central and South America, Tibet and others, we must look at what are the overall culture realities of these countries and their ways of living now!

"God is a man-eater, and so humans are sacrificed to him. Before humans were sacrificed, animals were sacrificed, because those to whom they were sacrificed were not god."
Nag Hammadi Scriptures Page. 170 Gospel of Philip by Marvin Meyer (2007).

The God I know, is the Creator not a destroyer and taking life away in His name is an abomination. The Father/Mother of all taught us through His Emissaries to love your neighbour, brothers and sisters and all His creations, including ourselves. So anything that was not, is not and will not be within this statement does not come from the Holy of Holies, the Most High!

Before I left Peru I gave my thanks to Pachakuti, Sachamana, Otorongo, Serokenti, Condor and Pachamama and all the Munay Ki archetypes, which brought me into this path where I am today. The Peru experience gave me more insight and confidence to write this book and prepare me for my next trip to Australia!

Chapter 26

The Power of Prayers

After Peru I experienced new downloads every day for the next couple of weeks and with an increased intensity. I was meditating daily and eventually the new Names I had been receiving stopped coming, so I was able to focus on feeling the vibration of each of the Seventy Two Names I learnt, chanting all of them and whilst regulate my breathing and feel their vibration within. One day I was focusing on the Light around me, created by visualizing a Golden Light or Prana while chanting the Seventy Two Sacred Names, I saw with my inner eye all the molecules organising one with another to form a face.

I pray daily using the Lord's Prayer adding the Name of the Father, Mother, Son and the Seven Spirits of God "YHWH" in it. When I pray repeatedly the Light from above descends through my crown chakra and travels along to the centre of my body. Sometimes, I can see colours, originally this was mainly green, but later became glowing golden white light that expands through out my heart. This is a Pillar of Light and helped release my soul from his binding through the clicks and cracks within my brain.

> *"A thousand will fall on your side and ten thousand at the right hand but it will not come near you".*
> *Psalm 91:7 Holy Bible*

During my prayers and also meditations I feel a gravitational pressure accompanied by the cracks and clicks as the Light descends flooding first into my head, my heart and some days throughout my entire body. It is very powerful, loving and liberating on its completion.

Since the beginning, I felt that praying was balancing my chakras. Because shear volume of energies I had absorbed during my meditations and experiences, my physical body was trying to adjust itself with the flow of these energies, causing me intense pains in my left shoulder – to the point that it could be difficult even to move my arm. The sensation that had been exerting pressure on my left side of my brain and inner ear was so strong that sometimes created it dizziness, especially in the morning when I got up.

Slowly, through praying and meditating, I was balancing these energies inside my body and the pressure within my inner ear got less and less. The pain gradually disappeared following the opening of other internal channel within my brain, but it was a big barrier to overcome.

It was late May and I was praying for my grandmother who was very unwell and unable to move. I was asking the Lord if this was her time to go, then to let her go in peace without any further suffering and when I was praying to the Light I felt strongly that my prayer was been received.

My grandmother was a very strong person. She was an ardent believer and a follower of the Evangelic Church. She lived living in the countryside and, I believe, she was suffering the effects of solitude and depression. Over the last couple years she had lost all sense of logic in her mind, hate and anger was taking her over. Her mind was creating scenarios in which people she loved were being unkind to her and these delusions were flooding her emotional state with anger, resentment and hatred. When her mental condition worsened to the point where she was a danger to herself and those people around her, the psychiatric doctor who was called recognized the symptoms of dementia and prescribed drugs to calm her down. This doctor likened her condition to the battle of Samson and the Pharisee, whose intention was to destroy all the people around him and himself. The drugs made her sleep, in other words within her she could not fight anymore and in a matter of a month she could no longer move, eat, or even speak. Her condition was rapidly deteriorating, but when she was taken to hospital, the doctor told my relatives to take her back home as there was nothing more they could do for her and that her condition could last for weeks. She was in a state of semi-coma.

When my sister told me of the grave situation, I knew I had to go to Sicily and try to help my grandmother. My brother wanted to come too, so together left a couple days later. We arrived in Sicily late at night, around midnight and went straight to see her. Her eyes were open but her breathing was laboured and her body was like a tiny parcel of skin and bones. When I sat next to her bed my mother came along and put my grandmother's hand in mine, I was amazed at how soft her hand was. I talked to her for a while holding her hand, which was very difficult for me because I had never really been in this situation before; but I knew I had to say what I was meant to say.

I told her who I was, that she was ready to leave this world and not to be scared. I asked her to invoke Jesus and she was right when she was saying to me that Jesus is the Way. I told her, if she called Jesus, He will send His angels from Heaven to come and collect her, and lead her to where there is no further suffering, only peace and love. Then I got out her Bible, which she had read thousands of times, and started to read the Gospel of John for a bit. When I looked into her eyes, I saw that she was overwhelmed by all of this, perhaps because I was the last person she would have expected it of. When my eyes got too tired to read, my brother read a part of the Gospel to her, then my sister and my cousin, each in turn, read to her from the Bible. So we all had a share in this event which from a very sad moment, became very emotional and brought us all together in a wonderfully peaceful environment. I left her side after a while, but I told her I would be back, and I went to my parent's house to take a shower.

By the time I finished my shower, the phone rang and it was my uncle telling me to get back quickly, because it was looking like the time for my grandmother to pass away. I dressed hurriedly and returned to her house, where she was rapidly fading away and, after a few minutes, she was gone.

That same night when I was lying in bed, I saw two souls come to where I was sleeping and hover around for a while. I felt the love around me and then they went. I do not know who the other soul was, but I was certain one of them was my grandmother. Prayers made from the heart are always listened to and this was not the only time that my prayers had been answered.

As I said previously, for me prayers balance our essence and activate the Pillar of Light. In Qabbalistic terms it is the Pillar of the mildness which balances our positive masculine yang with the feminine negative yin, making these two forces merge and became one. So prayers to God are important if we want to bring balance to our inner and outer universe. They will activate Faith, Hope and Love into our life.

Also, I believe the Lord's Prayer, the one Jesus taught us more than two thousand years ago, is a very powerful prayer. Jesus gave this prayer for a reason. In fact behind the words of this prayer there are many mysteries. First of all, through this prayer the plan of God is revealed and we really bring God into our life on Earth!

When I pray, I feel the intensity in my crown chakra, and I see and feel this Light coming down, surrounding first my face and then my entire body. In doing this, I let the will of God guide me for what is best for me and for all the people and creatures around me.

Often when we desire and ask about what we want instead of what we need, we bring more unbalances into our life. We confuse want and need and we only see life from the perspective of our five senses and we cannot see further, so we ask for things or events that take place because of our present condition or situation. But sometimes that present condition or situation, which can be uncomfortable or hard to accept and deal with, holds lessons for us to master thus allowing us to proceed forwards, permitting our soul to progress by the learning of our lessons, preventing us from becoming trapped in the same cycle of events, that become harder and harder to cope with. Our physical, mental and emotional bodies dictate what we think we need. That is why I do not agree when people tell me to visualise what I want and the universe will bring it to me. By visualising something we want or we think we need we could create more unbalances around us or elsewhere and we could go away from the tasks that God wants us to perform, during this incarnation. People think because they state their wishes from the point of light they believe is the right way for avoiding unbalances, but from my experience there are many lights, and sometime we don't know the difference between light and Light. They all appear bright to us, so it can be difficult to recognise the real one amid the fakes. The fall of Sophia is our proof! Only by meditating in what the Light or light is bringing, can one recognise which one is which! This is another reason why the Sacred Names were given to purify the light. By praying, we allow the Divine to enter into our house and He/She knows what it is the right thing that we need, both for ourselves and those around us.

I use the Lord's Prayer because it is a direct link to the Most High!
I have included the power of the Name in my version of the Lord's Prayer below:

Oh YHWH (*"Yahweh". This Name has been revealed by our ancestors and through the Sacred Scriptures, This Name is also called Tetragrammaton representing Fire, Air, Water and Earth and includes: the power of the Father, Mother, Son and the Seven Spirit of God who have created the universe were we live and they are the Elohim.*)

Who art in the Heavens (*He is from the many heavens that oversee us so He is not on Earth*)

Holy is Thy Name, Thy Kingdom come and Thy will is done on Earth as it is done in the Heavens (*Invoking Him by the Holiness of His Name, praying for the new Earth already made in the Heavens to come and replace the old Earth, and to bring His Will on Earth as already existed in the Heavens. Earth is mirror of the higher Heavens; the difference is that Earth is battered and unbalanced, because it is dominated by forces that follow the Will of ego and not the Will of YHWH leading us away from the plans of God.*)

Given us this daily needed Bread, (*Love and Light these are the needed bread, our weapons to transform ourselves and be one with God, and we need them everyday in order to overcome these unbalances forces*).

Help us to forget the debts that other people own to us, so all of our debts can be discharged. (*It is the power of forgiveness: by forgiving each other and ourselves, we* let all the negativities go, otherwise they have an hold on us. This is asking for help to clear our karma, in order that we can accomplish our mission on Earth without the need to reincarnate anymore.

Through hatred, resentment, anger, and fear, we bind ourself with limitations, indwelling with sufferance, depression and insecurity these are states of imprisoning for our soul and they will keep us in a very low consciousness state of mind, with a poverty and survival attitude! And if we do not let go, with this state of mind, new karma will be added to the existed one, because the wrong thoughts, emotions, words, and actions, that we have manifested by the result of not letting go, we will be kept in the circles within circles of negativities, far from reach our true Self. Forgive and you will be forgiven.

If we forgive from our heart we are set free to proceed for our evolution. We need the help of YHWH through His hierarchies of Light to give us the strengths to forgive and give love instead of hate. Do to the other what we would aspect that the others do to us)

Shield us from the tempter snare, that are too great for us to bear, and when they come give us the strength to overcome. *(Without the help of YHWH we cannot overcome the tempters and they will try their best to make you fall. Only through the help of YHWH we can receive the strength to overcome fears and temptations. The Lord's Pray is a direct link between us and God.*

Amen *(This is an acceptance of the power of YHWH and confirmation of His Will in us, because we are still under a free-will system. It is the power completion and command. We are limited without the help of YHWH, we are imperfect and incomplete without Him in our life).*

After the prayer I say this mantra below, which I also invoke when I feel under attack or need to clear away negativities. This is the highest form of thanks you can give to God and to release any form of negative influences within you.

Kodoish, Kodoish, Kodoish Adonai Tsebayoth
Kodoish, Kodoish, Kodoish YHWH Tsebayoth
Kodoish, Kodoish, Kodoish Elohim Tsebayoth

Holy Holy Holy is the Lord the God of Host.

The Lord's Prayer and also, as I later understood, praises and repentances through the Psalms are an essential part for the realization of God within and without of us. When we pray we should focus our mind on the meaning of the words, so Mind, Soul and Spirit are all At One Ment. Behind simple words, there is the unlocking of codes, which have been carefully placed to create a resonance that opens new Gates and Thresholds to new dimensions! We need to pray and praise daily if we want to bring The Living God into our life.

Jesus taught us is that we do not need to go to a church or to use a priest as a mediator to pray or speak to God on our behalf. We can pray to God anywhere, at any time. If we pray from the heart and have Faith, as I have said at the beginning of this chapter, our prayers are always listened to.

Chapter 27

The Environment Around Us

When I am at home I create with my routine of meditations, prayers, mantras, affirmations, calling in my guides and higher vibration music, a balanced environment. Through my experience, I know how a balanced environment feels and when I go to new places, I immediately notice the difference. I believe:

"KNOWLEDGE IS POWER, IF YOU KNOW YOU CREATE YOUR OWN REALITY IN HARMONY WITH GOD!"

The places where we live are made mainly by our thoughts and emotions. Places like airports or other public places in different countries are good places to measure the level of energies within the country.

"A donkey turning a millstone walked a hundred miles. When it was set loose, it found itself in the same place. Some people travel long distances but get nowhere. By nightfall they have seen no cities or villages, nothing man-made or natural, no powers or angels. These miserable people have laboured in vain."
Page 170 Nag Hammadi Scriptures Gospel of Philip by Marvin Meyer (2007).

When we visit any new environment it influence our mental and emotional state in a good or bad way. It all depends on the result of the sum of each individual level of consciousness, which means the most common, the most in number and we as individuals are part of the overall consciousness.

If we live a life full of fears, lies, sufferance, anger, hate, and lust, and these feelings are the most common within people of the same environment, this will be the reality of that environment. The sum of our thoughts, emotions, words and actions makes an overall consciousness creating a level of vibration energies. The higher the vibration, the more likely we can live a happy life and feel good with ourselves, the lower the vibrations means that we are likely to have unbalanced and more problematic life situations.

Just as blood gets oxygen from the lung with a process called diffusion (where the gas goes into the liquid by a gradient pressure and forcing itself in or out through membranes), so our outer consciousness in which we live is absorbed into our essence - our membrane - separating the outer consciousness with the inner consciousness. The strength of our inner consciousness determines if it is made of higher principles or lower principles, which, in turn, those will determine how much of the outer consciousness will be absorbed into our inner consciousness.

"After the Savior had said this, he continued again in his dialogue, saying to Mary, 'Listen now, Mary about the word you have asked me: what compels a man to sin? Now then, listen: when a child is born the power in it is weak, and the soul in it is weak, and also the counterfeiting spirit in it is weak; in a word, the three together are weak, without any one of them perceiving anything, whether good or evil, because of the burden of forgetfulness which is very heavy. Furthermore, the body itself is also weak, and the child eats from the sustenance of the world of the archons, and the power attracts the portion of the power which is in the sustenance [that is, of the power which is the Height]; and the soul attracts that portion of the soul which is in the sustenances [that is, of the soul which is in the mixture]; and the counterfeiting spirit attracts to itself the portion of evil which is in the sustenances and in its desires. On the other hand, the body attracts into it the matter from the sustenances, that is unconscious. The destiny [moira] in contrast takes nothing from the sustenances, for it does not mix with them, but will leave the world in the condition in which it came. But little by little the power and the soul and the counterfeiting spirit grow, each one of them perceiving according to its nature: the power becomes conscious and learns to seek after the Light of the Heights; the soul become conscious and learns to seek after

the region of righteousness which is mixed, which is in the region of the mixture; and the counterfeiting spirit becomes conscious and learns to seek after evils and desires and all the sins. In contrast, the body perceive nothing unless extract the power from matter. The three immediately develop awareness, each according to its nature, and the avenging receivers assign the servitors to accompany them and witness all the sins which they commit, taking note for the method and manner of how they will chastise them in the judgements. And after this the counterfeiting spirit observe and takes notice of all sins and evil which the archons of the great Heirmarmene have commanded for the soul and makes the soul to do them. And the inner power moves the soul to reach for the region of the Light and the whole Godhead; and the counterfeiting spirit tempts the soul and continually forces it into lawless actions, all its passions and sin, and holds steadfast to the soul and is antagonistic to it, forcing it to perform all this evil and all these sins. And the counterfeiting spirit spurs on the avenging servitors to witness all the sins which it will make it [the soul] do. Furthermore, when it will rest in the night or in the day, it agitates it with dreams and desires of the world, making it desire all the things of the world. In a word, it shepherds it to do all the things which the archons have commanded for it, and it is antagonistic to the soul, making it do what it does not want to do."
Third book ,Page 607-610, Chapter 111:282-283 Pistis Sophia A Coptic Text of Gnosis with Commentary by JJ and Desiree Hurtak

The Enemies are inside as well as outside of us, and through what we see, hear, feel, say and do, sins are made, and chains are cast into our souls!

Inner consciousness will be upgrading or downgrading all depending on our decisions. It will be harder for somebody to maintain higher principles in a lower principles environment; the survival state will kick in, bringing fear and hate which will be likely to prevail. Nature teaches us that it will always try to achieve a state of balance.

Most countries have a level of vibration that is determined by the people living in it and by the karma assigned to the country, and this establishes the overall consciousness of the country. Things like the media – television, magazines, radio, music, etc. – have a strong influence on our life. They manipulate us from the outside, trying to take control of who we are on the inside. They tell us what we want, what to do, where to go, how to behave and how to speak! They are telling truths, but sometimes these are the truths of few or none and they are imposed on our minds and emotions!

"Blessings on the person who has laboured and found life."
Saying 58 – Nag Hammadi Scriptures Gospel of Thomas by Marvin Meyer
(2007).

And if we try to stand for our higher values, events will be created that will test our strengths. This is done to keep us down and under control, because we are seen as a threat.

Now, when I visit different countries, I view my surroundings with different eyes, I applying the same rules mentioned in the previous paragraphs. I study the behaviour of people: what they watch on television, what kind of music they listen to and the cultural conditions where they live. I am looking at the result of what has been fed through their senses and what has been created by people.

It is always easy to blame individuals for our state of being e.g. like politicians, public officials, employers and of course they will have a bigger price to pay; because of their individual positions, they bear the responsibility not only of their own souls, but also of all the others souls that they take control of with their doctrines and actions.

But, the real truth is nobody else is to blame than our self!
We must take control of our life and be responsible for our actions!

In the consciousness, which overall has produced lower vibrational energies, the majority of the people within the country think about themselves and will thus have a very unbalanced country dominated by fear, anger, lust and lack of respect for nature. There will be lots of greed, corruption and a high level of criminality; it will be a much disorganised country with most of its people struggling to survive, no one accepting responsibility for their actions and all of them blaming each other. This creates inconsistencies, false realities and a bad Karma, so strong that it will be very difficult to clear.

Conversely, if the majority of people within a country think about the good of the community, we will have a more balanced country: no stray animals, public services clean and reliable, plenty of parks and green recreation areas, strong conservation a healthy respect for nature, little crime resulting in very wealthy country where it is more likely that truth, fairness and consistency prevail.

"His followers asked him and said to him, 'Do you want us to fast? How should we pray? Should we give to charity? What diet should we observe? Jesus said: do not lie, and do not do what you hate, because all things are disclosed before heaven. For there is nothing hidden that will not be revealed and there is nothing covered that will remain undisclosed."
Saying 6 – Nag Hammadi Scriptures Gospel of Thomas by Marvin Meyer (2007).

I have been to places where the environments are well balanced, each individual having contributed in the creation of it with their consciousness and the positive result is easy to see. We make who we are and where we live! It is our individual consciousness (thought, emotions, words and actions), which creates our being, our home, country and our world!

Nowadays, I see more and more struggles in the lives of individuals, couples and families. We are challenged everyday; sometimes it feels a hopeless situation, which ends up in desperation and wrecking us.

It is like a boat that is sinking, there is big hole and the water is coming in all the time and we spend all our energy trying to bail the water out from inside with a bucket to avoid to be submerged. But we are making a mistake, if we want to save this boat as we need to concentrate our effort and energies on closing the holes, to stop the water entering!

We need to pause take a deep breath look around us to see where we are and start to look for those holes. Then we will realise that the problem starts from within and what there is within will be replicated outside us! If within there is confusion, anger, lack of time, intolerance, poverty etc. This will be our external reality - *The Law of Attraction, Universal Laws* - and in the life of a couple or family environment, it becomes a battleground. Playing the blaming game is not the solution; rather we need to make an effort to tidy up our inner house first. This could mean changing our habits, mode of doing things, ways of saying things and trying to re-enforce the weakest parts of ourselves. When we try our best to do so, we must remember that the other people around us are also doing their best both consciously and unconsciously. Slowly we will become in harmony with ourselves and only then can we be in harmony with our outer world.

Within the Universal Laws I mentioned earlier, I have found so much wisdom. When I look at the reality of where we live, I believe that if everyone will know and apply these laws in their life, this world will be already Heaven.

I found this affirmation very powerful in one of the books of Dr. A Villoldo, I did change it slightly by adding the Sacred Name, and every morning when I get up and go for my walk after my prayers, this is what I affirm:

> *Yahweh is in front me (and I visualise Gold Light in front of me)*
> *Yahweh is behind me (visualizing the Gold Light behind)*
> *Yahweh is within me (visualizing the Gold Light within)*
> *Yahweh is Below (touching the ground where you are and visualizing the Gold Light below)*
> *Yahweh is above me (looking at the sky visualizing Gold Light)*
> *Yahweh is surrounding me (turning your head at 360 degrees and visualizing the Gold Light around)*
> *I walk into Yahweh kingdom (walking and visualizing you, I walk into the Gold Light)*
> *And because of this we say I AM THE LIGHT OF THE WORLD!*

Anyone anywhere can say this affirmation and everywhere, it helps to stay positive and strengthens our soul.

Chapter 28

The Age of Changes

It has been predicted by ancient civilizations, sensitive individuals and in many books, that our planet is changing drastically. It has been written that from a the third dimension planet that we currently inhabit, it is going to jump into the Fifth dimension. This is due to the position of our planet in relation to our universe and is called the Process of the Equinox - a phenomena occurring about once every 26000 years, when Earth position closer to the Great Centre Sun of this universe.

"Jesus said: The heaven and earth will roll up in your presence, and whoever is living from the Living One will not see death."
Saying 111:1-2 Nag Hammadi Scriptures Gospel of Thomas by Marvin Meyer
(2007)

"The Universe was moved at the presence of the Lord of the whole Earth; the Aeons was troubled and in suspense because it had seen that which it knew not. The King of Glory was seated, He divided matter into two halves and into two parts. He fixes the borders of each part and taught them that they came from One Father and from One Mother."
Page. 69 The Gnosis of Light A Translation of the Untitled Apocalypse contained in the Brucianus Codex by F Lampugh and R.A. Gilbert (2006)

This means a higher consciousness, so higher vibrations, and we are already feeling these changes; global warming, political controversy, bankruptcy of countries, family and social instabilities, widespread disease, conflicts and wars in sacred areas. People are faced with making important choices in one way or another, and it is these crucially important choices that will determine the intensity of this transformation. These impending changes are not only about Earth and the ones above it, but also about us!

"But someone may ask, 'how are the dead raised? With what kind of body will they come? How foolish! What you sow does not come to life unless it dies. When you sow, you do not plant the body that will be, but a seed perhaps of wheat or something else. But God gives it a body as he has determined, and to each kind of seed He gives its own body"
1 Corinthians 15:35-38 Holy Bible

Earth will carrying on living but we humans need to adapt ourselves to these changes, otherwise we will not be able to survive. We need to change; need to evolve into a new species for the time to come, from Neanderthal, to Homo Sapiens to Homo Luminous or Adam Kadmon that is to say the new Adam who has regained all his birthrights - the garments that were stolen at the beginning of our time.

"It is sown a natural body, it is raised a spiritual body; if there is a natural body, there is also a spiritual body.
So it is written: The first Adam became a living being; the last Adam, a life giving-spirit. The spiritual did not come first, but the natural and after that the spiritual. The first man was of the dust of the earth, the second man from heaven. As was the earthly man, so are those who are of the earth; and as is the man from heaven, so also are those who are of heaven. And just as we have borne the likeness of the earthly man, so shall we bear the likeness of the man from heaven."
1 Corinthians 15:44-49 Holy Bible.

I sense the changing around, but also I see and feel the changes within me. I chose the future, I chose to embrace the Universe and keep it alive within me!

When I started feeding my rites or seeds at the beginning of my journey, I did not know what I was doing. But later on, I understood; it was all to build my Light Body. My meditation, prayers, affirmations and mantras, my spiritual trips, the changes I made in my daily life by embracing my decisions, the way I think and my studies, all of these things contributed to transforming myself. In a little more than three years, I became a different person. I embrace it, I feel and see the Light inside. I close my eyes and I see Light. From time to time my face becomes illuminated with Light, and my body within during my meditation is full of Light. And because of the *law of attraction - Universal Laws*, I am bringing in more and more from the Outer Universe, through downloads from the Heavens into my crown and thence the whole of my body.

"The next few years will be like the snake or other reptiles shedding their skins. The transformation into the future will turn the destiny of the planet Earth back to the Divine. The Masters will rejoice with the children of the Light, and inheritance will be that of the gold."
Page 5, We, The Arcturians by Dr. Norma Milanovich with Betty Rice and Cynthia Ploski, (1994)

I experience clicks and cracks mainly within my brain and sometimes through other parts of my body, like it wants to expand. The clicks and cracks are the smashing of the ties and chains imposed by the fallen hierarchy. I feel new parts of my brain have been activated, it has been said by scientists that we humans use only a few percent of our brain capacity and I could not agree more. Spirituality is the future for us, but the spirituality that I mean is the reconnection with the Living God.

"To those who ran unto him and adored Him He gave the place at the right hand, and gave them Life for ever and ever and immortality. He named the place on the right 'The Land of Life', and the place on the left 'The Land of Death'; He named the Earth on the right 'The Earth of Light' and the Earth on the left 'The Earth of Darkness'; He named the Earth on the right 'The Earth of Repose'; and The Earth

*on the left 'The Earth of Sorrow.' He placed boundaries between them, veils so that
they might not see each other; He gave many Glories to those who had adored Him
and gave them dominion over those who had resisted and opposed Him."
Page. 69-70 The Gnosis of Light A Translation of the Untitled Apocalypse
contained in the Brucianus Codex by F Lampugh and R.A. Gilbert (2006)*

I experienced also what I call Uploads, Light from within going out from
the crown chakra. My soul and my Spirit want to ascend to higher realms
and became one with my Higher Self body. The body, through the
emanation of Light from the pineal gland, creates new forms of hormones
which is changing our DNA and are changing our body, instructing each
cell with a new curriculum. To intake this new form of energy or "Prana"
I hear the changes in the sounds emitting from my essence, what people
call the music of the spheres, which is becoming an ever pitched higher
note, and from many becoming only one sound. I have put all my effort
into transforming myself into the Light and with Love all my old self is
gone. When old thoughts come to me with past scenarios, I bless them and
release them into the Light, in order to remove all old data which does not
serve me anymore; as their purpose is only to make us heavy, anchoring us
in this dimension. This is why I understood the power of forgiveness -
when we forgive with the heart, anything which has bothered us will go
and we experience a sense of relief, like a burden has been lifted from us!

*"listen, I tell you a mystery: We not all sleep, but we will all be changed - in a
flash, in the twinkling of an eye, at the last trumpet. For the trumpet will sound, the
dead will be raised imperishable, and we will be changed".*
1 Corinthians 16:51-52

I decided to speak about my experiences and share them, because I primly
believe things are really changing for all of humanity and time is running out!
We need to store within us enough Light, so when the Groom comes we
need to shine forth and welcome Him. The Groom is the outer Garment of
Light is the Christ. I have seen my outer Garments on several occasions and

I have had just a very small experience of how it feels, but even through this small morse, I cannot find anything on Earth that I could compare it with in greatness. It was shown to me to give me a small glimpse as to what can be achieved with and what it is the aim. I only needed to find my way back.

It has been written: seek and you will Find! We must never stop seeking because by seeking we will find!

I never stopped seeking, even though I wasn't sure what to expect or what I was looking for, but I knew there was something beyond my imagination, and I wanted understand what it was. This has been the motivation which has kept me going for the last three years, with faith and hope, throwing myself vigorously into this path, and refusing to stop until I have found what I was meant to find. We are close to our global changing and the main change indeed starts from within all of us.

"Jesus answered: 'watch out that no-one deceives you. For many will came in my name, claiming, I am the Christ' and will deceive many. You will hear wars and rumours of wars, but see to it that you are not alarmed. Such things must happen, but the end is still to come. Nation will raise against nation, and kingdom against kingdom. There will be famines and earthquakes in various places. All these are the beginning of birth pain."
Matthew 24:5-8

Apostrophe to Zion

I will remember you, O Zion, for a blessing;
With all my might I love you;
Your memory is to blessed for ever.
Your hope is great, O Zion;
Peace and awaited salvation will come.
Generation after generation shall dwell in you, and generations of pious shall be your
ornament.
They who desire the day of your salvation
Shall rejoice in the greatness of your glory.
They shall be suckled on the fullness of your glory, and in your beautiful streets they
shall make tinkling sounds.
You shall remember the pious deeds of your prophets, and shall glorify yourself in the
deeds of your pious ones.
Cleanse violence from your midst; lying and iniquity, may they be cut off from you.
Your sons shall rejoice within you,
And your cherished ones shall be joined to you.
How much they have hoped in your salvation,
And how much your perfect ones have mourned for you?
Your hope, O Zion, shall not perish,
And your expectation will not be forgotten.
Is there a just man who has perish?
Is there a man who has escaped his iniquity?
Man is tried according to his way,
each is repaid according to his deeds.
Your oppressor shall be cut off from around you, O Zion,
And all who hate you shall be dispersed.
Your praise is pleasing, O Zion;
It rises up in all the world.
Many times I will remember you for a blessing;
I will bless you with all my heart.

You shall attain to eternal righteousness,
And shall receive blessing from noble.
Take the vision which speak of you.
Be exalted and increase, O Zion;
Praise the Most High El El Elyon, your redeemer!
May my soul rejoice in your glory!

Vermes, G., The Complete Dead Sea Scrolls in English Revised Edition, Penguin Books, London, 2004, Page 311-312. Dead sea Scroll Hymns and Poems.

Chapter 29

Re-visiting the Crop Circles

In the month of July I was thinking to sort out the trip to Australia, but also I felt strongly I should re-visit the crop circles in Wiltshire before the end of the season. The experience of the crop circles of the previous year was remarkable and left me with imprints in my consciousness.

Our friends from other dimension have been trying to help us since the beginning of our evolution on this planet and they have been cooperating with higher kingdoms in order that our transition to the Aquarian Age was delivered as it has been written thousands of years ago. Last year the trip within the crop was purely introductive, re-confirming to me their existences and their active work on Earth. Since then, I knew I had to go back, and understood the time of my return was drawing close as my Guides had given me an idea when I was supposed to be there.

This time I went alone to visit the circles from 6th to 9th August staying at a B & B in a village near to Stanton St Bernard, one of the places where the phenomenon of the crop circles are to be found and this trip was an adventure from the start.

I was on the lookout for new crop circles. I had a map of the area, which my friends Ann and Graham had given me the day before I left home and from this I knew where to find the Silent Circle Café a meeting point to see the photographic images of all the current crop formations and their positions on the map, together with location instructions and updates for the fresh ones.

When I arrived at the café on the Saturday morning I was surprised to learn that most of the crops had been harvested. So I really didn't know where to start, but while I was in the shop trying to get some inspiration, I met two Polish guys living in the United States. They were also somewhat bemused, so we decided to join forces. It was much easer for me to concentrate on the driving while my new friends navigated using the map.

The first circle we visited was close to the village of Alton Barnes. It was not very big circle compared to the others but it contained what looked like some Aramaic writing in it. The day was cold and wet, and we found only a few other people there when we arrived at the site. I promptly walked round the circle trying to understand the flow and directions of the energies and I wanted to find the most suitable place to attune with the vibrations within the crop. I closed my eyes and with my inner eye I saw colours, mainly green and violet.

After this circle, we went to see the next formation on our list, which was very close, just on top of the hill. This crop formation was a pattern of circles all aligned, one after the other, from the biggest to the smallest in diameter, the first circles had some wings extending sideward. As I approached it, I didn't feel any vibration at first but, when I went within the middle of some of the smaller circles, I felt the flowing of energies within. We spent only a short time there before moving on to our next formation, which my co-driver was very excited to visit.

Following our map, we looked everywhere but we simply couldn't find it. We spent most of the morning looking for it and we started to question our reference on the map. I insisted on returning to the café to check it out, and be sure we had plotted it correctly on the map - which we had not! In fact the mark on our map was on the wrong field. We marked it correctly and went out again.

This crop formation was located in a place called Whitefield Hill, on top of a big hill and not far from where we were looking originally. It was a beautiful square formation with a circle in the middle giving a three-dimensional effect. When we arrived there were only two people from Norway, who they were just leaving the formation, when one of them started chatting to me, asking me if it was real or not. "And who makes them?" One asked, I answered him, based on my experience, for me they were genuine and that this verdict was not only based on the physical evidence, but also upon vibration of energies it was emanating. I'm not sure if he believed me.

After the Norwegians left, I start to attune with the formation in the same way I did before - by standing in the centre of the formation, letting the wonderful energies flood all my essence. While I was focusing with my inner eye on the Light, a group of people started to come around close to where I was and I began hearing metallic noises, like the rattling of metal cooking pots. I could hear them just one step behind me talking; distracting me from what I was doing. They were also foreign. I thought for a minute that maybe they were going to have a barbecue just behind me and this idea made me smile. But, thank God, these 'pots' were singing bowls, and soon they started to chant the Name of YHWH and it was beautiful! They produced a very healing sound, a balancing of energies and, with my inner eye, I saw a very bright emerald green the experience lasted maybe an hour or more; my whole body was vibrating intermittently. When they finished, I thanked them for their contribution. We chatted for a while and I learnt they were a group from Spain, travelling to Wiltshire to see the crops. It was late afternoon when we left. I said goodbye to my Polish friend and I returned to my bed and breakfast for the night. I was very happy with the achievements of that first day.

The next day was a Sunday, the Crop Circle Café was closed, so I had no way of finding out if there were any other new crop circles. I decided to drive to Salisbury, to a burial chamber I remembered from last year. Graham and I went to see a formation in this area and we had also visited the ancient chamber. It was a quite interesting experience.

The sun was shining when I arrived at the burial chamber. It was a very lovely day, but there was nobody else at the site. I sat near the entrance, again feeling the vibrations of the place, which were extremely powerful. I stayed there for more than an hour being recharged. From where I was sitting I could see the imprint of the Yin and Yang, last year's formation amid the freshly growing wheat in the field in front of the burial chamber.

I decided to return to the Alton Barnes area, where I parked at the top of a hill near the well-known White Horse formation. While driving, I had spotted a big formation that I was drawn to go and see straight away. I was so exited. In the meantime my partner rang to tell me there was a report of a new crop circle in the vicinity of Alton Barnes and I was convinced it was the one I had spotted.

I made my way there and was soon inside this new formation, walking along the trim line from where I could see lots of people coming towards the crop circle from the other side of the field. This formation was again made up of several large circles, with wings on most of them and a crown on top of the first circle. I decided to sit in one of the middle circles and attempt to attune with the vibration emanating from the formation. The energies were flowing around the formation and the main colours I saw in this crop circle were pink and white.

It was only later on that I realised this crop was the same crop I had seen the day before. People from the café wrote report saying it was a fake and they were convinced it was man-made, but the formation I saw had changed from the original shape and was different to how it was before my first visit. Some people were saying it was half man-made and half made by aliens and I could not agree more. This crop pattern had definitely been partly re-made by aliens; I had felt a strong vibration coming from it. In fact, some of the crop was broken at the stems in a messy way, whereas the new addition was perfect. When I felt it was time to leave the formation, I made my way out along the trim line, and it was then that I saw a couple of people crossing the field below, stamping on the wheat to reach the formation and damaging the growing crops underfoot. They were jumping through the wheat creating their own way into the formation, without using the trim line. I saw the farmer with his quad-bike driving along the track next to the field where the formation was, shouting to these people to use the trim lines. They paused for a few seconds, then glared back at the farmer and carried on jumping and stamping, making their way through the wheat towards the crop formation, completely ignoring his request. The farmer stopped near me and shook his head in disgust. He was a nice man and we chatted for a while. I told him I was sorry about these couple of people damaging his wheat and I was telling him that before, while I was there, I had seen maybe more than 30 people, all walking in the trim line and being respectful of his land. He replied by telling me that these few morons were spoiling it for everybody! advised him to voice his concerns to the café owner and to get his message posted on the relevant website, to ensure that visitors to the site are aware of how to behave and respect the Country Code. There wasn't even a donation box for the damage done to the wheat in this field!

I went to have my lunch on top of the hill of the White Horse. It was a beautiful view from there; the sun was shining on the colourful landscape and lots of people were out walking. Also, I was enjoying the energies around the White Horse. Looking down, I saw that one field had just been harvested. Later, I understood this was the field where the new formation had appeared during the night and it had been harvested early in the morning. I saw the pictures on the café computer in the afternoon and it was a fabulous formation which they had managed to get some aerial shots of, even while it was being cut.

While sitting near the White Horse I met a couple with a very energetic dog and we started to talk about the authenticity of the crop circles. I was again, through my experience, able to share the truth with them, but on this occasion I found strong resistance to my views as they were fervent christians. I could see in their eyes their fear of the unknown, even though the husband was more keen to open his mind to new possibilities and realities of existence, but fear was making them judge and condemn. For me this is how religions try to manipulate and dominate humanity both historically and also in this day and age. If new awareness does not fit into their consciousness, it is denounced as evil and in past times it was put to death!

"You see the speck that is in your bother's eye. When you take the beam out of your own eye, then you will see clearly to take the speck out of your brother's eye."
Saying 26 – Nag Hammadi Scriptures Gospel of Thomas by Marvin Meyer
(2007).

Anyway, it was this couple who told me about another crop formation appearing nearby, in the Stanton St Bernard area, very close to where I was. so I thanked them and went to look for it.

After looking for an hour, I finally found the correct location and. When I reached the crop circle late in the afternoon it was full of people of many nationalities. I found the crop formation because I saw the crowd from the road and when I reached the site, I noticed most of the people, did not care about the crop vibrations or trying to feel the energies. Most of them were there to gossip and chat very loudly and the result was polluting the vibration around the crop! I stayed there for a while but I could not feel anything. People were taking photographs and there were planes and helicopters flying around like flies. I decided to leave.

"Why you have come out to the countryside? To see a reed shaken by the wind?
And to see a person dressed in soft clothes, like your rulers and your powerful ones?
They are dressed in soft clothes, and cannot understand truth."
Saying 78 – Nag Hammadi Scriptures Gospel of Thomas by Marvin Meyer
(2007).

The next morning was my last day in Wiltshire and I went out early to re-visit formation of yesterday afternoon where I was hoping to find a quieter environment than yesterday. I parked the car close to the road and, to my relief no one was there and I went along the trim line trying to find my way into the crop formation, but I could not see it. I went back and forwards several times, but still I could not find it!

I realized, I was not centred enough so I stopped, breathed in deeply and tried to relax. My inner guidance told me to look for vibrations, so I walked along the trim line, crossing other trim lines perpendicular to the one I was following, but I was still not feeling anything. So I carried on and, finally, I reached a trim line where I started to feel some tingles in my hand. I turned left, and after a few minutes of walking I still could not see anything but the vibration was getting stronger and stronger, until I saw a steel pole with a donation box attached to it. Only then did I see the formation and entered into it. It was beautiful and only inside I could appreciate the vibration around. The crop formation was small but stunning, an intricate pattern. It was in the form of a spiralling shell circle, representing a Golden Mean. I attuned easily with the gentle vibrations around me; before reciting the Lord's Prayers. Whilst absorbing the beautiful energies surrounding me; I received some downloads into my crown chakra, then, while I was there meditating, I heard someone approaching so I opened my eyes and saw it was the farmer emptying the donation box. We had a conversation and also he asked me if I thought the circles had been created by aliens. My reply were the same; as before and, harbouring no doubts, I told him of my experiences.

I asked him if the donations covered the cost of the damage to his crops. Despite the generosity of some people, he said not and he would be happier if the crop circles stopped occurring on his land. I told him people come from all around the world to see the circles and advised him to have faith and perhaps it may be a good idea if next time when he harvested the field to leave the area of the formation uncut for people to continue to visit them and he may be surprised by what he might learn, whether the donation box proved profitable or not. He told me the previous year on his field a hummingbird formation had appeared and, for the first time, the donations had almost covered his costs. The farmer was very friendly, another nice man.

I decided to leave the crop circle and move on, as a helicopter had been annoying me for a while and more people were starting to come along. I knew my purpose for being here in Wiltshire and I was not yet satisfied. I knew there must be other crop circles in the region and I needed to go and visit them too.

When I went to the café, there was no news of any new formations and the one of yesterday morning had been harvested by the farmer that same morning. I was there trying to get some ideas, so I asked the owner of the café if he had any news and he told me there were two more strange formations close to one I had just seen that could have been there for a couple of days, but had only just been discovered. He thought they were genuine for there was nothing to suggest they were man-made. He warned me they were very small with no complex symbols or signs, just spiral rings. They reminded him of those seen in the beginning, when the crop circles first appeared in Wiltshire; and went on to tell me what he and his team do when the crop formations appear, which was to go to the formation and evaluate it using only physical evidence. He told me he himself was not able to sense any vibrations from them, rather he inspects the physical evidence such as the bending of the wheat, consistency of the formation, possible tracks made by people to the crop and so on. He has done this for many years and he recognises straight away if it is a fraudulent or genuine. I saw the pictures on his website of the little formations he had described to me and there was a simplicity about them. I asked him how I could find them (because I know it is not easy to see them, even if you find the field) and he explained to me where they were and that I would find a member of his team studying them if I went there straight away.

After debating what to do, I decided to get the map and mark the field and left although I was not too sure how to find it! I followed the directions given by the café owner and kept my eyes open for the field. and in the middle of it I saw a man taking measurements and making sketches. I parked my car next to his and went to meet him. As I neared the formation I could see only the one little track made by the guy who was there; it seemed that no one else had yet been there. I spoke with the cafe'team member and informed me of another bigger crop circle in the next field reiterating that these circles were genuine. When he left, I sat along inside this little circle for a while. The energy flows were very strong and reflected in my inner eye were many eyes and symbols as I felt the sensations of downloads running through me. I stayed for a long while and, because the energies were still coming, I didn't know whether to leave or stay even longer. I tried to listen to what my inner voice was saying and it told me to move on to the next one. I didn't want to move, but in the end I forced myself to leave.

The next one was a more difficult to locate and even though I went into the trim lines and looked for it I could not find it anywhere. I carried on looking around without success, when my partner rang and told me about a new crop that had just appeared near Horton village. I asked my inner guidance if this new crop circle at Horton Village was the one I needed to go to see to fulfil my journey here? I was getting mixed messages because I was not in line or relaxed enough to listen properly. I tried again to breathe deeply and carry on my questioning. I nearly left the field, but again, my inner voice told me to stay where I was and try to find the formation, so I persevered and at last I saw a little clearance - once I got closer I could see it was there! I went inside and it was clear that nobody had yet been here. The crop circle was totally intact, so I went in and around it, I picking up the strong energies emitted. The formation itself was in the shape of the letter Q. I stopped and tried to attune with it; the Light brilliant and intense bringing with it symbols and downloads I could not see properly because of the blinding Light when the sound of a breaking tree branch made me open my eyes. I asked if this was the sign for me to go. The answer was yes!

I asked about the new formation and the inner voice within told me I didn't need to go to see it, but I decided to go and see it anyway. After the last crop circle I felt a sensation of achievement and had enjoyed the challenge of finding them. Satisfied, I left the field and drove back to the café to get directions for the latest appearance.

On reaching the field, I saw a lady walking up through the field but by the time I had had reached the trim line the lady was already back down the hill. I asked if she was looking for the new crop formation and she said yes, but informed me it has been cut by the farmer already I was surprised, because the field was not harvested yet so I went into the field anyway where could hear voices in the distance and saw people walking away. I looked around and I saw the place where the formation had been; the farmer has cut only the formation, leaving a large bare patch in the middle of the un-harvested field. I thought it was a good lessons for me, a sign to be more faithful to my messages as well as a confirmation that I had achieved what I was required to achieve. While I was there looking at the clear space where the formation had been, I head a soft noise. I turned around and saw two beautiful deer hiding within the crop just a few metres away from me – such gentle creatures with beautiful eyes.

I left Wiltshire feeling vibrant, although my shoulder was very painful from the huge amount of energy I had absorbed in the last three days. The sensation was almost as if I was coming back from an intense spiritual workshop. I realised how tired I was when I was back at home that night, but I was full of Light.

The experience in the crop not only raised my vibrations but also introduced new elements to my meditations, as well as influencing my dreams. I had a dream about the crop circles, and *it is all about Love and Light*, which is what we need to master in order to raise our vibrations to go through the thresholds of the third and forth dimensions and be ready for the new dimension in which planet Earth is going to be placed. During my crop re-visiting I had been subjected to several tests. I talked with different people and I shared my views. Truth, faith and hope, were the main tests I had to confront.

Before I had left home to see these formations, I was instructed by my Guides that only three crops were going to mean something to me and I had the dates of when they were supposed to appear! But when I was there and I could not see them, I began to doubt the accuracy my source, in the end my guidance proved right, I found the three formations on the correct dates too, resulting in raising my vibrations to the point where my face was being illuminated for the next eight days!

Several times during my meditations and prayers, I saw beautiful mandalas, composed of intricate patterns made up of what looked like marbles and I was going through them. It was my first encounter with mandalas in my meditation and I didn't know the meaning of them. I was also given a Star of David and was guided to draw it out, revealing a multitude of geometrical figures, within and without of the symbol. I was guided to use my crystals and stones, the ones I found named in the bible to surround me during my meditation sessions. Initially I formed a square before evolving through a series of geometrical shapes, before ending with a triangular formation. I noticed, all the patterns I made with my stones were within and without of the Star of David, and I was always placed within them. The pain in my left shoulder and arm was very intense, and during this time I had dreams/vision of me fighting the devil with the help of Michael and Jesus.

I was concentrating on cleansing my chakras in sequence, from the base to the crown letting them spin faster than the speed of light, and moving onto the next only when I was seeing an emanation of the correct clean and pure colour related to that individual chakra. Through this method that I realised doing that the spinning was energising all my body. The heart chakra was regulating all the Light; the Light I had been accumulating during my meditations and the crop-circles experience was been re-distributed all around my body, much in the same way that our physical heart pumps blood around our bodies to supply our cells with nutriments.

During this time, I experienced strange things within my body, the first of which was spiritual beings talking to me via my left ear I could hear him clearly. Next, a very strong upstream of inner Light forced itself through, creating an acute pain and burning sensations in the left inner ear area. Sometimes both during my meditation and after, when my rising energies from within were travelling to my brain, they were accompanied all the way with a sequence of clicks and cracks from both the right and left brain hemispheres and with a strong pressure upwards like a volcano that was going to erupt at any second. When the energies reached the middle of my brain, in the area where the pineal gland is located, a big bang occurred akin to a cap blowing off. The first time this happened I was worried that something within my brain had been damaged by this internal pressure, but then I realised it was the final opening to reach the upper levels. I was reaching more and more where I could see with my inner eye the state of my inner body to be all bathed in Light. I could see with my inner eye the Light emanating throughout my physical body, with no clicks and cracks, and I understood the old writings as well as the new sayings – we will reach the point to be a being of Light, and this was happening to me. It is real! But I could only hold this state for an hour or so.

I noticed Grace was coming more often, surrounding me with peace and love; the sensation on my body was like being cloaked in a refined silk. I started to listen to high vibration music CDs which I had bought from the Academy of Future Science (Dr. Hurtak's website), and which were filled with sacred expressions and Names. I played them during my meditations as they were helping me to raise my vibrations even more. With this music, the Light I was seeing was more vibrant and colourful than ever, with pyramidal shapes.

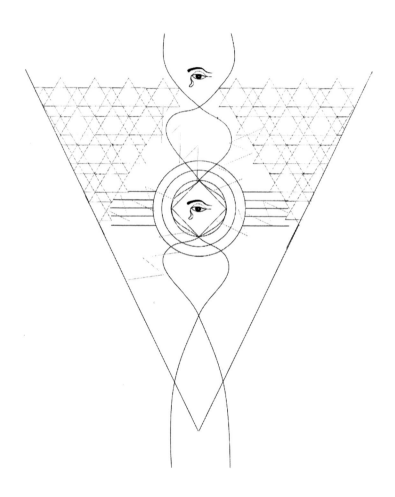

Chapter 30

My Tanzanian Battle

It was the mid-October 2010, and my trip to Australia looming, but before my departure, my partner and I went on a short holiday to the National Game Reserve of Selous in Tanzania. This is an area where I have had strong spiritual battles previously and, of course, this time was not going to be any exception!

We went to a different area from were we normally go; it was a unique small tented camp in a concession where hunting was allowed until very recently and still around this oasis of respite for animals hunting was highly active!

One of the main sources of revenue of Tanzania is trophy hunting, a multi-million dollar business. The government issues land concessions within this beautiful area of the Selous National reserve to private companies or influential people. It is a large area located in the southern part of the country and should be a paradise for the wild life, whereas instead it has been decimated by the hunters and poachers. People come here from all around the world to kill a lion, leopard, elephant or any other form of wild life they wish to have the pleasure of killing! It is all about how much money the hunter is willing to pay! They claim it is strictly controlled, with only the weakest and oldest or the surpluses being chosen to be victims on the list of the trophy hunter. This so-called strict control by government officials is highly questionable! I have been travelling in Tanzania for quite few years now, and I do have a fair idea of how this trophy hunting works. This is a country where the lower selves are very active. Horrific stories abound, for example shooting an impala, leave it prey hanging on a tree and hide in the bush waiting for the leopard to arrive to shoot it on sight. The hunting guides are supposed to monitor the activities of the hunters on behalf of the government, but a handsome illicit payment invariably ensures that the guides turn a blind eye. The temptation is too strong and principles are too weak. This is clearly not a sustainable situation for the continuing good of the environment, and this place will be depleted for everyone in a few years time.

The reality is, when I went to see this eco resort in Selous, I noticed straight away the difference in animal behaviour between this park and the parks where the hunting it is not allowed. The animals on this side of the Selous are so scared. They live in constant fear and they are always on the run, wary of the hunters with their high-powered rifles. I was happy to visit this place because I could see that the people managing it had made a conscious decision to change from hunters to protectors. They were now determined to protect, preserve and embrace the wildlife and not contribute to destroying it. They had realised that the rampart, uncontrolled killing was not going to be sustainable, because it was decimating the entire ecosystem.

People say that photographic tourism also has an impact on the natural behaviour of the animals, and this is true, but the difference is that when you track and get close to the animals to admire their beauty and the sight of their vibrant and harmonious natural life, it is vastly satisfying. We are happy to see animals enjoying a balanced and healthy lifestyle, which in turn activates a part within us called unconditional love - an expansiveness and infinite state of mind, essential for us to evolve as human beings. This differs from the goal of hunting tourism which is to admire the beauty of dead matter, receiving pleasure through tracking it, instigating fear and terrorising the animal community by through the random slaughter of their members. All of this factors indicate a contractive and limited state of mind, giving to the perpetrator a finite awareness of a matter without life!

For me, killing any animal for the sake of passion, sport and ritual is a SIN!

As I said before, sins are blockages within us; they release new karma into our consciousness, making it more difficult to reach higher realities, truths, peace and love, in order to accomplish the Will of our Eternal Father on this planet. Furthermore, in the last ten years it has been an increase of extortions made by us human beings to the African eco-system, the influence or invasion of the Chinese into the African continent that has accelerated the process of auto-destruction.

Flying from Dar Es Salaam to Selous, I had a strange painful experience which at times was unbearable. When we landed at the camp, it took few minutes before I started to feel better. I went out with the game driver and saw that it is indeed a beautiful place.

We were staying in this camp for only five days, then returning to London I was staying in a hotel for a night before flying out to Brisbane, Australia the next day. But for those entire five days I was not feeling well. It started the first night; I felt under attack by lower energy forms and I could see them around me in the room. My energy field was healthy and also my chakras, were working fine, but my inner body was in trouble. I had difficulty even to breathe. I didn't go out for a couple of days on the game drives. I had a strong fever; I was sweating profusely and my brain activity was very high. People in the camp were very worried; they thought I had caught malaria.

I knew I had to fight it. I could not succumb to this illness now and compromise my next trip; it would not make any sense. The Australian trip was where all my guidance was leading me to go. There was a doctor staying in the camp and she offered me some drugs. I thanked her, but since my spiritual awakening, I have refused the intake of any drugs, especially anti-malarial ones. I wanted to face what was going on; something was telling me it was all related to my trip to Australia.

I was still meditating in the afternoon which gave me enough Light to face this battle. I was telling myself it would not make any sense if I got malaria now. My meditations were very powerful, I had again Grace coming to me and in the stillness I was being shielded with Peace and Love. I had lots of Faith. I didn't sleep for three days. My brain activities were too high to sleep; I was experiencing high speed thoughts. I believe also my vibration was high, producing heat around me, making it unbearable for me even to breathe. I saw with my inner eye lots of negativity around me especially in the faces of grotesque spirits. I decided to fight all this but, when I got too tired just striving to protect myself while observing these happenings. I went within and I invoked the help of Michael; I embraced His sword and started to fight and purify whatever was in the dark and I started to transmute it into the Light. To my surprise I was managing to improve matters; where was dark became Light. Then my guides told me to ground it all to the centre of Earth, and when I started to ground all these energies downwards, it was amazing; like a river in full flow downstream and then suddenly it stopped. I was commanding my chakras to spin at full speed and my attention was on my heart chakra; it was playing up - trying to stop spinning. I focused on my heart chakra to keep it spinning at full speed, while all this was happening I saw so much Light with my inner eye becoming more and more intense, I needed to re-distribute all the Light from the chakras to my whole body. I was getting restless. The following day I remained in my tent and tried to rest, trying to slow down all this activity because my brain was hardly able to cope with it. I was also monitoring my thoughts which were of a lower nature; I was definitely under attack! Over the last few weeks I had been monitoring my thoughts, trying to keep my vibration high in order to be ready for my spiritual journey to Australia and at this moment I was finding it very difficult to control them! I could not afford to get malaria and leave this world, not after all I had been through. There must be more to it.

Faithfully, I prayed to YHWH for help, asking him to remember me, not to forsake me and later in the afternoon after my last meditation, things began to calm down. Within, I felt protected; I knew He always keeps His promises. By the third day I was feeling much better. Aware that I was dehydrated, I drank a lot of water and that evening I joined the others for dinner. It was a relief for everyone.

But when I went back to my tent I knew the battle was not yet over and that night was another episode I will never forget! Spiritual activity was very high within the tent, I could see so much Light from the inner eye, and was bombarded by thousands of colours all together to and also bright jewellery-like pieces shining in the Light. It lasted for hours during which I was very unsettled and restless, my breathing was very shallow again. I tried to slow down my breathing by taking deeper breaths while lying on my back with my legs straight. I started to see rays of golden Light spiralling skyward and I went with it reaching the highest I could go, where I needed to be. I stopped there and it was the Heavens, all beautiful bright blue Light. Then, in a split-second, I had a sensation that something had departed from me, released from within me. I felt so light and in a wonderful state of well-being. This was the same sensation I'd had when I began my journey nearly two years ago. My spine felt like a strong steel bar. Amid this sensation of lightness, I felt strong and untouchable. I thought something major was happening. I was very happy, because I knew I had managed to overcome this battle.

The next day I felt very good and my health improved rapidly, apart from a bit of a chesty cough. I was managing to do my meditation daily and also go out on the game drives. Towards the end of this trip I had beautiful encounters in the wildness and I discovered some very interesting places. But most of all I was ready for Australia!

Chapter 31

My Australian Mission

It was early in the morning of the 28th of October 2010 when I landed in Australia. During the long flight I tried to meditate by staying with the Light and listening to the CDs I had bought from the Academy of Future Science, to keep my vibration high. Before setting foot on Australian soil, I asked my guides to protect me during this trip. After my experience in Tanzania a few days earlier I didn't want a repeat of it Down Under.

I had a few worrying encounters, like when I was asked to produce my yellow fever certification. But, thankfully, my partner had reminded me to take it with me. Without it, the Australian authorities could deny my entry. Also I still had a chesty cough and coming from a country where there is a risk of malaria and yellow fever meant that they could put me in quarantine. Luckily I found the certificate very quickly and the immigration officer allowed me through.

When I reached the hotel it was too early to check-in into my room. I was told I had to wait until mid-day, to get the use of the room, but they kindly let me use another room to have a shower. I was exhausted but at least the shower woke me up a little and I was able to leave my bag in the hotel while my room was being prepared, so I went into one of Brisbane's nearby parks, to while away the rest of the morning.

While in the park, I used the time to do a few practical things. I activated my new SIM card on the phone and booked a boat trip to see humpback whales for the next morning. I was struggling to remain awake, but finally the time came and I returned to the hotel. I had another shower and went straight to bed.

It was around 7:00 pm when I started my meditation and for most of my stay in Australia this became was the time for me to meditate. At first I had difficulty trying to connect with the Light, feeling like something above my head was stopping the Light flowing through to me, but I was patient and did not start to chant the Names before the Light was well anchored within! Eventually the Light found Its way through, then I was guided to chant the Sacred Names.

During my first days of meditation in Brisbane I had the same sensation of barrier and resistances within and without of my essence trying to stop the flow of the Light within me, but with patience and focus on the Light I managed break through to clear these barriers. I felt the power of Grace surrounding me again with Peace and Love. My face was glowing with Light very intensely from within and I had a strong visions; I saw a mandala filled with brown and real earthly colours together with some of the aboriginal symbols and animals, similar to other visions I had through out my stay in Australia. When I meditate I always have some past experiences appearing from nowhere which I normally acknowledge, give my apologies before blessing and releasing them into the Light, a practice I continued on this trip. I had important insights, telling me about the power of channelling the Light and chanting the Names of The Most High, and by that doing it I was participating in the activation the surrounding areas, infusing the powers of the Names into this sea of consciousness made of molecules, raising the vibration of Mother Earth, reconnecting her with her original link, the Supreme Source! I understood, chanting the Names and the Lord's Prayer, from the point of Light I was activating all the codes of The God Force, within and without, bringing the Living Father onto Earth with us. This is what I had been doing all along and this was my mission revealed for Uluru Rock! These thoughts were telling me whereabouts I needed to be at Uluru Rock.

After Brisbane, I went to Cains, a large centre for tourism north of Brisbane, which gave easy access to explore the Great Barrier Reef. I went there because I booked a 5-day trip on a live-aboard boat to dive the Great

Barrier reef. Staying on the boat was a very interesting experience, but it was very difficult for me sit and meditate, so I lay in bed listening to my CDs and staying with the Light. The diving package I bought included 4 dives a day, but I could not dive manage this, as I felt my body was not fully recovered from the experience in Tanzania, so I limited my self to an average of two dives per day and only one when I felt very weak and cold. My focus was Uluru rock!

On 4th November, 2010, I caught a flight from Cains to Ayers Rock and flew over the outback, which simply was stunning. On the plane, I sat in a window seat, eager to see the landscape of the outback beneath. An American woman, who was seated next to me, asked me if I would give my seat to her husband who was seated just across the aisle from her. It was a very strange question to ask, so I looked her with a smile and said I was sorry, but I really wanted to admire the outback from the air. She said that was okay and then, during the flight, she was very kind to me, offering me her fruit after hearing me tell the flight attendant that I was a vegetarian to which the attendant replied there was no vegetarian dish for me on the plane. She offered me her apple, and her husband's apple as well, which I thought was very nice. I thanked her and jokingly said, "An apple a day keeps the doctor away." She replied straight away to me saying, then it was not good for her because her husband was a doctor! So we had a laugh. She later asked me why I was going to Ayers Rock so I told her it was a spiritual trip. I realised she, too, was seeking answers when she told me she was trying to find the meaning of her existence in this world. She was reading and following advice, even trying to meditate, but she was finding it very hard and struggling with all the concepts, so I gave her some book recommendation and advised her to read them with an open mind like a small child.

While I was flying above the outback I saw and understood why the Aboriginals painted with such a diversity of colours and lines of dots and darker spots. I was seeing all below me, even the forms of their sacred animals – and also I understood why, when I asked at the jewellery shop in Cains, which crystal stone would represent Australia, she replied without hesitation, "Opal." Flying over the outback I was seeing salt lakes and, water holes and with the sun's reflection, they were like big opal stones, so beautiful, reflecting all kinds of rays and colours.

I landed at Ayers Rock resort, which is 40 minutes drive from Uluru Rock and more than an hour from the Olga Rocks. Somebody on the bus on our way to the resort was telling us that this year the Anangu (the community of the local aboriginal people, which numbers about a couple of hundred people) the traditional owner of the land of Ayers Rock National Park, bought the resort of Ayers Rock in a hundred million dollar deal and that they were celebrating the event while I was there. I thought it was wonderful that the local people had acquired full ownership of their land and the infrastructures built by the big enterprises.

When I arrived at the resort I went to the information centre where I bought my passes and tickets for access into Ayers Rock National Park. The first thing that was struck me was the rich redness of the sand desert. I planned to get up very early the following day and catch the first bus at around 4:30 am to see the sun rise before going straight to Uluru Rock.

The next morning, I followed my plan with the intention of finding the place where I needed to be for my meditation. I was on time and the most incredible thing was that I was alone all the way. There were hundreds of people in the sunrise area a few kilometres away, but at the actual Uluru rock I was on my own!

Through my inner guidance once I found the place where I needed to be for my ceremony and meditation, I opened my Sacred Place, invoking my Master and Guides to help me on this task. Intense and beautiful birdsong continued throughout my meditation. I had the usual blockage or resistance so I needed to stay with the Light long enough to open up any blockages and let it flow freely within all my essence, before I could chant The Sacred Names of the Most High. After a while, when I felt I transformed and opened my blockages, I was given the go ahead to chant the Names.

I felt safe and undisturbed, even from the insects and flies. I knew again I was in the right place. I chanted the Names from east to west, facing all the lengths of Uluru. After I finished chanting the Names, I had many visions of paintings in old caves from the ancestors, seeing a deep red colour for a while, then a rainbow coloured kangaroo alongside I saw lizards and ants leaving their tracks. I was with the Light, but I felt I could not expand the Light outwards; there was too much resistance. So I stayed with the Light for a while longer reciting the Lord's Prayer ten times. Then an emerald green colour flooded my vision and I could feel the heart and all my essence softening. I asked if I achieved what was meant and the answer was yes although I decided to stay a little more with the Light while I had managed to have such a strong connection. I tried to be the Light and with persistency I was an expansive Light. And soon I was One with the all and Uluru. I stayed for a moment longer, then I let the emerald green Light stay within. I opened my eyes quickly, because I felt a sensation of burning on the back of my head. I wondered if I was burning my head like I did in Brisbane, but I did not care. I wanted to finish and do properly what I have been planning to do for months and now it was the time to manifest that. By now I had been meditating at Uluru was about two hours.

When I finished my meditation, I packed up all my altar and I started to walk around the base of Uluru. It took me more than five hours to go all around the rock, but it was worth every minute. Some of the cavities in the rock had more vibration than I had previously encountered. The eastern part of Uluru is mostly a sacred area, where even nowadays Aboriginal women and men use this areas for their own ceremonies deep within the caves. By the end of my walk I was exhausted. Despite the sweltering sunshine I did not perspire at all as it was a dry heat causing my sweat to evaporating straight away. I felt the usual fulfilment of accomplishment!

The next day, I travelled to the Olgas, another spectacular place. I was guided to the right place where, I was again on my own opening my sacred space calling the directions before reciting the Lord's Prayer ten times. On completing the task I closed my sacred space with my thanks and blessing. Just after I finished closing my sacred space people started to come around.

My thought repeatedly were being drawn to the Aboriginal communities; both their beliefs about and also about the war for the soul, which they believe is held at Uluru. I discovered that they are really struggling to share their beliefs with people of other nationalities, because they are a very secretive people. Even amongst themselves they keep many secrets because of their laws. They kept their culture alive because of their secrets, passing knowledge by word of mouth only to those they thought worthy of it and never in writing. These laws left and decreed by their ancestors, are the foundation of their society and daily life. Most of them live under the jurisdiction of their native laws which are enforced by their tribal elders. These laws include respect for sacred places and spirits, together with rules on how to live together. Each tribe has its own beliefs and protectors, called by different names, but they all acknowledge the same One Creator. The laws demand respect for their lands; they have their own individual territories which each tribe feels a strong connection with, but their land is more than merely a place where they live, much more than a home. Their land speaks to them and advises them how to find food and where best to hunt. Tribes from other areas must not cross into the territories of other tribes without first seeking permissions. It is all about bringing balance, prosperity and peace amongst the collective society and those who disobey these laws are punished. It is very rigid and austere; there is no escape and serial offenders can be banished from the community. In their own way they have experienced what has happened in the west. They have connections with their spirits, some of which are good and some are not so good.

"The Pharisees and scholars have taken the keys of knowledge and have hidden them. They have not entered, nor have they allowed those who want to enter to do so. As for you, be as shrewd as snakes and innocent as dove"

They also believe they retain the original genetic human code, which has not evolved for thousand of years and like the Hebrew people, they believe in the promises of their laws. However I believe that without faith, hope, and love, without Christ, they are not in tune with the time to come! I believe that spiritual law is the foundation for faith, hope and love to be securely laid upon.

The sting of death is sin, and the power of sin is the law. But thanks be to God! He

People of every nationality, of course, have inherited and abide by laws devised by their ancestors but, these laws differ from the Universal Laws, which are not man-made. Only through Christ will we ultimately bring peace and salvation to mankind!

In the afternoon, while I was in the minibus, we passed by Uluru Rock before return to the resort I was busy admiring its colours and shape when I received an amazing vision:

A battle was raging on top of Uluru. It was like a battle of Titans and I saw a giant who I recognized as Archangel Michael with his sword fighting to conquer Uluru. I saw a huge monster coming out of Uluru, and other creatures with red eyes, all trying to fight back and escape when Archangel Michael brought his sword crashing down on them. Uluru become white. And these Monster and all his creatures they were cast out from Uluru and they were on the loose coming towards me as I was looking at them! This vision remained etched in my mind, even months after I returned from Australia.

The war in Uluru that the aboriginals are seeing is represented by the battle of the two snakes, the rainbow snake (Creator) and the black snake (Ego). They have been at war for a long time at Uluru (The Kingdom). I believe that it is time for Uluru to re-connect with the Heavens!

The day I was due to leave, I got up early and I went to pray at Uluru for the final time. I felt more vibrations then than on my previous visit. I walked around turning into the peace and beauty, I was again on my own for most of the time. I felt I had achieved all that I could possibly achieve here. With faith I was following my guidance without hesitation, even at times when I

"And there was war in the heaven. Michael and his angels fought against the dragon, and the dragon and his angels fought back. But he was not strong enough, and they lost their place in heaven"
12:7 Revelation -The Holy Bible

did not know exactly why I was doing it. But kept my faith and in the end I got my answers!

From Ayers Rock I travelled to Western Australia to spend a couple of days with my partner who had come, for a meeting. here I finally managed to have some more open discussions with a local Aboriginal. I saw him as the future of the Aboriginal people - more willing to share and embrace other cultures and realities. I told him we are all one!

In those few days I was guided to keep my Sacred Place open at all times wherever I went and to keep on meditating, even though I was finding difficulties and the usual resistance within and without myself. During this time I had a very interesting dream:

A builder planned the foundation and then placed a floor above it, putting the first tile and the last tile together at the very beginning, He was able then to connect all the remaining tiles, the Beginning with the Last, they will follow their own course!

"I am the Alpha and the Omega," said Lord God, 'Who is and who was, and who is to come', the Almighty." Revelation 1:8 The Holy Bible

During my short visit I saw a new generation the one and the same generation that has striven to introduce change through the channelling of high intelligences into their consciousess. This generation has tried to deliver the necessary Wisdom to embrace the needed Divine Love, through their dreamtime-visions and storytellers.

Chapter 32

The Calling for My Deliverance

On arrival back in the UK I was very tired from all the travelling and not sleeping so well but, while in the car from the airport I had intense downloads which lasted for hours rather than rest again, once home, I could not sleep that first night back due to the intense thoughts that were invading my mind, about how things really are and how people are influenced in their normal lives. I lay awake most of the night so I decided to listen to some of my high vibration music to relax. As I opened my eyes I could see and feel a swirl of energy fields in the room, indicating a strong spirit presence in the room, confirmed by a membrane located between my nose and up inner mouth making a clicking noise. Then a spirit figure appeared and I could see it with my naked eyes. As it became more clear, I asked who He was? He told me He was coming from the Brotherhood Of Light and He was here to help me and guide me. I welcomed His Light and energies. He told me about the veil and self-realization and that I was very close to accomplishment it. After this visitation I had strong visions of major cities breaking up and sinking. Strong energies started to penetrate me through the crown chakra, affecting the right side of my brain. At first they were very intense, among the most intense downloads I have had and were accompanied by strong filling the right side of my brain. This almost unbearable pain persisted, before it began to flow down to the left side of my body. I saw orbs of golden Light and I recited the

Lord's Prayer in order to take some of the edge off centralising the energies into the middle of my brain. After that I saw a myriad of colours everywhere passing through my consciousness. Little clouds of light were encircling me and I saw some alien beings, similar in many ways to those experiences I had at the beginning of my awakening. There came a moment when I realised that I needed to get out of bed and sit down comfortably to let these energies flow more freely.

"These 'whole light beings' come down through the artificial time warp zones and land upon the face of the Earth. And this is what the ancient beheld when they saw the pillar of the cloud go up before their face".
The Book of Knowledge: The keys of Enoch, Key 205:48 by J J Hurtak

Later that morning, I felt energies in my head and clusters in my back heart chakra which needed balancing out, so I achieved this by letting the chakras spin faster and faster until I could see the emanation of the brightest, cleanest colours coming from them.

I began reading *Pistis Sophia, A Gnostic Gospel by GRS Mead (1984)*, which I had been guided to read during my return journey from Australia. Pistis Sophia means Faith and Wisdom and is magnificently incredible book! It really is five books in one and speaks about the ministry of Jesus for an eleven year period following his resurrection. He was teaching his disciples all the mysteries and the teachings were a revelation to me meaning that here I found most of my answers!

I understood that Faith on its own is not enough; it is blind. It is only with Faith and Wisdom can we reach the Heights of the Heavens. But to acquire Wisdom we need Faith and there is no Wisdom without Faith!

In the following months I went into deep isolation. I was venturing out just to walk my dogs and doing some occasional food shopping. I was completely immersed in my studies. Receiving new Words and guided to a new Invocation, I was also under the attack of fallen forces trying to deceive me both in my dreams and in my meditations with the objective of trying to slow down my journey and derailing me from my true path. Fortunately I recognised this and with prayers, Sacred Names and Faith, I managed to transform what needed to be purified. I re-read and re-discovered some of my books, plus new ones for me was a time of discovering and receiving. During my meditations I was applied the new Words, by chanting them into the Light as I was trying to call in and activate my Garment of Light. I had dreams and visions revealing more mysteries and Words to me, but I was not ready; I was missing something.

So, my meditations for a good month were very different than my usual practise. I was now focusing on cleansing my chakras and purifing them. Which took me a long time and perseverance, I used the Words and Names to open up thresholds or gates of light, I followed a path in order to reach places which enabled me to receive another 19 new Sacred Names - a continuation of the first 57 Names that I had received seven months ago. The 57 new Names or Sacred Expressions thus become 76 Names. I did not understand at first: why 76 Names? And what is the meaning of them? Why?

All of this was granted by following my inner guidance during my meditations. The Names came this time with the language of Light; I saw them with my inner eye but I could not translate them. It was for my 'Overself' to translate letter by letter to me and again with Faith I went along with it. These meditations were very long and tiring; between opening the chakras and the Names it was at times taking more than five hours, as it was imperative I purify myself to enter into these places.

I was achieving the state of a complete purification by seeing and focusing on the colours of each chakra, letting them spin and going deeper and deeper until I felt a releasing and cleansing sensation on each chakras. When the chakra was completely open, it was like swimming in a sea of refreshing water; freedom without any resistance. As I cleansed each chakra, clicking and cracks were occurring, in my head centred around my pineal gland area in particular and my whole brain in general. I was reaching the status of a complete liberation within. I could feel, first a cold air sensation within the chakra, then in my body and finally filling the entire room. It was a beautiful sensation but very tiring.

I didn't understand fully the reason for all of this. I knew I could not carry on like this; my body was complaining because it was taking a lot of effort for my physical body to cope with reaching this stage of freedom for just few moments, infact the next day I was repeating the same steps again, as the chakras all needed to be cleansed once again. I was confused! To open each of them fully I had to be in a state of loving calmness, and to project only beauty in to what I was seeing. I had to endeavour to keep thoughts of frustration, tiredness and pain out because I knew from experience, if I allowed my attention to drift away from the chakras colours, I would not be able to make it to the last chakra. This state lasted for more than a week in the beginning January 2011.

Cleansing and opening my chakras was the first thing I had to do. It was a process of unbinding and releasing that was occurring through each of the chakras, but the main effect was felt within my brain, with more cracks than a clicks. It needed to be endured to retrieve the new Sacred Names!

Even after receiving the Names, my meditations continued to be intense and tiring. I started to clear each of my chakras, like I had done for the last month, but now my aim was only to unbind myself using this technique I had learnt, therefore it took more than four hours in each meditation session to achieve my aim. Then one day, when I was going through the some process again, something rather unusual happened. I had worked my way through my chakras following what had become my routine but, while I was focused on the violet of my crown chakra and letting flood my essence, unexpected I saw a brilliant white colour descending. It flooded all my essence and I was guided to stay with it until a very bright chrysolite colour descended again flooding my essence. This was followed by a brown, then a crystal clear diamond light and finally gold all of which descended from above and flooded both my inner and outer essences. On reaching the last stage with gold light I was guided to start to chant for my first time the entire 76 Names all together.

I continued to do these intense and extremely long meditations for about sixteen days, each based on the opening of the chakras, together with the chanting of the 76 Names, which resonated more like a mantra, the most common Name of which in is YHWH. This was terribly exhausting and without the help of my guides I would never have been able to achieve it. I learnt to focus on Mind, Body and Spirit and be At One Moment! Suddenly, after these weeks, the need to open and cleanse stopped as quickly as it had started! Only later did I understand that I had spent the month in the process of activating the 76 Names of my Tree of Life together with my upper 5 bodies with the chakras!

I continued devouring other books, and receiving other insights, applying them to my meditation. On the whole though, I was re-chanting the 72 Names and reading specific psalms from the Holy Bible. And this was the last time that I had to be focus on my chakras!

During the following year, through the use of my daily prayers, repentances, meditations and readings, I composed a song, singing it every day to praise the Most High. In prayers I was asking for His mercy and forgiveness for all my sins and to be granted with His Divine Wisdom, in order to be completed and so that I may know His Glory and fulfill His Will by bringing Heaven on Earth!

One day while I was praying, I realised after a dream that I had been robbed, I saw with my inner eye the image of a woman dressed in purple and blue garments coming towards me but, when she got too close an angel appeared in between us wielding a flashing sword preventing her from approaching me!

These were the days in which I fought my devil with the help of the Light in order to overcame and transmute him and regain my birthright - The Garment of Light!

The loud noise of the devil to Humility and to the rest of the Virtues
What is the power which may be no one except God
I, however, say:
"Any person who will have wished to follow me and my will,
I will give all things to that one;"
you truly, together with your followers have nothing which you are able to give,
because all of you
do not know what you are.

Humility answers
I together with my companions know well
that you are that ancient dragon,
who wished to fly above the Highest,
but God cast you forth into the abyss.

Virtues
We all, however, dwell in the highest places.

The lamentation of the same Soul repenting in the body
and invoking the virtues
O you royal virtues,
you are so splendid and so shining in the highest Sun,
and so sweet in those remaining faithful;
therefore, o woe to me, because I flee from you.

Virtues
O fleeing one, come, come to us,
and God will receive you.

The Soul repenting in the body
Ach, Ach, a fiery sweetness swallowed me up in sin,
and therefore I do not dare to enter.

Virtues
Do not be afraid nor flee,
because the Good Shepherd sought you as a lost sheep.

The Soul repenting in the body
It is necessary for me now that you lift me up,
because I fester with wounds
with which the old serpent poisoned me.

Virtues
Run to us,
and follow these footsteps in which you will never fall
with our companionship,
and God will care for you.

The Soul repenting in the body
I am a sinner who fled life,
I will come to you full of sores,
so that you may hold out the shield of redemption to me.

Virtues
O fleeing soul, be strong
and clothe yourself in the armour of Light.

The Soul repenting in the body
O all you of the royal army,
and you white lilies with rosy purple,
incline yourselves to me,
because I lived as a foreigner among you.
Help me in order that I may be able to rise up
in the blood of the Word of God.
O true medicine - Humility -
hold out help to me,
because pride shattered me with many vices,
placing many scars upon me.
I now flee to you:
therefore receive me.

Humility to the virtues
O all you virtues,
receive this mourning sinner with her scars

212

because of the wounds of Christ,
and lead her to me.

Virtue to the Soul repenting in the body
We are willing to lead you back,
and we are not willing to forsake you;
all the heavenly army rejoice for you;
therefore it becomes us to sing this musical performance.

Humility to the same repenting Soul
O wretched daughter, I want to embrace you,
because the greatest of physicians has suffered
harsh and bitter wounds
on your behalf

The suggestion of the Devil to the same repenting Soul
Who are you or where do you come from?
You embraced me
and I have led you forth,
but now in your turning back you confound me;
I, however, will hurl you down with my assaults.

The repenting Soul against the Devil
I knew all your ways to be evil,
and therefore I fled from you;
with these means, however, o deceiver,
I fight against you!

The repenting Soul to Humility
Whence you, o Queen Humility,
help me with your medicine.

Humility to victory and to the other virtues
O Victory, who conquered this one who is now in heaven,

hasten with your companions
and all of you bind this Devil.

Victory to the Virtues
O very strong and most glorious soldiers,
come and help me to conquer that deceitful one.

Virtues to Victory
O most sweet warrior
who swallowed the greedy wolf with rushing
fountain,
o glorious one who has been crowned,
we freely fight as soldiers with you against this
deceiver.

Humility to the Virtues
Therefore bind Satan,
o very bright Virtues.

Virtues
O our Queen, we will be obedient to you,
and we will fulfill your precepts in all things.
Hildegard Von Bingen's Mystical Visions page. 382-389
Vision Thirteen (1995)

During this time I had other insight and visions but most of all I had been
guided with Humility to be in Faith and Hope and carry on knocking to the
door of Wisdom.

A certain man with great possessions had two sons.
The youngest son grew tired of life at home and said,
My father, pray divide your wealth and give the portion that is mine to me,
and I will seek my fortune in another land.

The father did as desired, and with his wealth the young man went into a foreign land.

He was profligate and soon had squandered all his wealth in ways of sin.

When nothing else remained for him to do he found employment in the fields to care for swine.

And he was hungry and no one gave him aught to eat, and so he ate the carob pods that he was feeding to the swine.

And after many days he found himself and said unto himself,

My father is a man of wealth; he has a score of servants who are bountifully fed while I, his son, am starving in the fields among the swine.

I do not hope to be received again as son, but I will rise and go straight to my father's house, and I will make confession of my way-wardenss;

And I will say, My father, I am come again; I am a profligate, and I have lost my wealth in ways of sin;

I am not worthy to be called your son.

I do not ask to be received again as son, but let me have a place among your servants, where I may have a shelter from the storms and have enough to eat.

And he arose and sought his father's house, and as he came his mother saw him while yet a great way off.

(A mother's heart can feel the first faint yearning of a wandering child.)

The father came, and hand in hand they walked a down the way to meet the boy, and there was a, great joy.

The boy tried hard to plead for mercy and a servant's place; but love was all too great to listen to the plea.

The door was opened wide; he found a welcome in the mother's heart, and in the father's heart.

The father called the servants in, and bade them bring the finest robe for him; the choicest sandals for his feet; a ring of purest gold for him to wear.

And then the father said, my servant, go and kill the fatted calf; prepare a feast, for we are glad;

Our son we thought was dead is here alive; a treasure that we thought was lost is found.

The feast was soon prepared and all were merry, when the eldest son who had been serving in a distant field and knew not that his brother had returned, came home.

And when he learned the cause of the merriment he was offended, and would not go into the house.

His father and his mother both besought him tearfully to disregard the way wardenss and folly of their son; but he would not; he said,

Lo, all these years I have remained at home, have served you every day, have never yet transgressed your most severe commands;

And yet you never killed for me a kid, nor made for me a simple feast that I might make merry with friends;

But when your son, this profligate, who has gone forth and squandered half your wealth in way of sin, comes home, because he could do nothing else, you kill for him the fatted calf and make a wondrous feast.

His father said, My son, all that I have is yours and you are ever with us in our joys;

And it is well to show our gladness when your brother, who is near a dear to us, and who we thought was dead, returns to us alive.

He may have been a profligate; may have consorted with gay courtesans and thieves, yet he is still your brother and our son.

Then Jesus said so all might hear: He who has ears to hear, and heart to understand will comprehend the meaning of this parable.

The Aquarian Gospel of Jesus Christ (1911), Section xvii, Chapter 144:3-30

Chapter 33

Connecting with the Light

From the many experiences I had throughout recent years I started to write some basic points as a reminder of how to increase the Light within us. These I now list below:

> It has been said, "There are many paths but only One Way to the Light" – I understood later in the year, this only one way is the Christ!

The rest is all a manipulation of the self-willed (ego)!

> "A teacher is also a student, and the student is teacher, an enemy is also a friend and a friend is also enemy."

In writing this book I am disclosing some of the meanings of some mysteries I learnt through my experiences. Which I believe can help us increase our ability to be closer with the Living God.

We must learn to monitor our thoughts, emotions, words and actions; I understood this was my very first lesson and also to treat all others, including the plants, animals and stones, the way that we would like to be treated ourselves!

Then, learn to pray, repent and praise the Most High every day, because we are clay without his help!

The invocation I was guided to write is both a praise and a prayer, to establish a link and create a Sacred Place, an essential practice before starting a meditation. Encoded within this invocation is what we want and need to achieve.

Before commencing a ceremony it is important to burn a stick of incense in the room (be aware some are not so genuine; they are full of chemicals and will give you a headache, so find the genuine ones). Do not eat for at least two hours before meditation.

Invocation

Oh YHWH, Father, Father of all Fatherhood, you Unending Light, Unutterable One, Unspeakable One, Unnameable One, Ungenerated One and Self-Generated One, Unmovable One , Uncontainable One, you Truly are our only God and Eternal Father. Hear us, be merciful to us, forgive all our sins, the ones we know and the ones we don't know. You are slow on anger and quick on forgiveness, release us from the tempter snares, the ones that keep us bound in these worlds of limitation, Oh Father deliver to us Grace and Love, let them abide with us. Let Thy Glory be manifested through us.

We humbly praise Thy Names for the fulfilment of Thy Will. Save us, through the infinite emanations of thy Divine Presence. Let us understand the mystery of the first commandment – I am the Lord, your God who brought you out of the land of slavery, you shall have no other gods before me – And from this commandment your Son our Saviour Christ Jesus descended and gave us the way to regain our lost birthright. And through your Son, Joshua, we will be delivered!

Give us The Strength, The Mercy, The Love, The Knowledge, The Understanding to master The Wisdom, which is necessary to be with Thy Glory. Let us work with your myriads of Angels, Archangels and Lords with their Orders: The Malachim, the supervisors of the Universal Laws, The Ishim, who assist us to evolve and be ready for the higher dimensions; The Elim, the sustainers of the vibrations of the spheres; The Hashmalin, who Judges; The Seraphim, the Guardians of Consciousness; The Erelim, the Covenant Keepers; The Ophanim, The Messengers Of Light, The Cherubim, the keepers of High Intelligence; Metatron, The Creator of Outer Light, Melchizedeck The Great Receiver of Light; and the Archangels of the direction :

(Facing the 4 direction invoking their presence)

South– *From the South Archangel Michaelilu, Oh Mikaelilu, Prince of the Heavenly forces, who fought and fights to protect us and release us from all the negative influences of the lower forces of darkness…*

West – *From the West Archangel Gabriel, Oh Gabrielilu who also fought and fight to raise our vibrations with His songs of Light, let us hear your trumpet of Victory…*

North – *From the North, Archangel Uriel, Oh Urielilu, Creator of the inner Light, who light up our souls let them shine as stars into this darkness…*

East – *From the East Archangel Raphael, Oh Raphaelilu, who deliver us from the evil and bring to us the fruits from the Heights…*

And to the Saviour Yoshua-Yahweh-Jesus who brought compassion and forgiveness with the Power of Love! Who opened the gates of Light for us, and delivered to us Peace and Truth.

Oh Lord Adonai you are our Refuge and Fortress, Elohim Misgabi, Oh Almighty One, Ani Shaddai spread your wings and protect us, because we have made the Most High El El Elyon our tent, our God Yahweh in whom we trust .

And, thank you for giving us the songs to praise our Most High El Elyon:

Kodoish Kodoish Kodoish Adonai Tsebayoth

Kodoish Kodoish Kodoish YHWH Tsebayoth

Kodoish Kodoish Kodoish Elohim Tsebayoth

Holy, Holy, Holy is the Lord, The God of Hosts!

And we now declare this place a sacred a safe space so be it! (visualizing a circle of fire that encompasses you, and you are within). Amen, Amen, Amen and Amen!

After the invocation is accomplished, sit in a lotus position or normal sitting position, maybe on a chair or a pillow in order to raise your body a little from the floor. The second step is to try to relax and attune with the energies, then ask the help of your guides to come within and help you from within by guiding you through the whole process. When you have finished the meditation, you should always give thanks!

Our mind is manipulated by our ego, which can create scenarios which deceive us, try to seed fear within us and other harmful distractions. We must try our best to keep our mind free of entanglements, try to free ourselves with the expansive power of Love and the power of freedom of Forgiveness; never give up. It is not easy, but when we recognise our opponent in the fight, overcoming them becomes easier and we realise what we are trying to achieve - our aim is to let Grace come within. Remember there is a light and Light, through using the Power of the Sacred Names of the Most High, we will reach the point of beginning to purifying the light, which will in turn will start to permeate us. Without the Sacred Names or Sacred Expressions this light will deceive us so we need to transform it to Light. Soon, the focus must no longer be upon the Third Eye chakra, but the consciousness must be moved to the alignment of the crown chakras with the heart chakra. By this time we should already be following the inner voices, which try to give us direction.

Again, use discernment and ask questions! If I am not sure which energies or spirits are surrounding me I say the Mantra mentioned earlier. Be aware and awake.

By starting to journey in other dimensions, with guidance, we will be taken to places where the Holy Spirit will deliver to our essence "The Gifts". Most of the time I saw with my mind's eye, but I didn't understand what I was seeing or if I was receiving anything - but I knew I was seeing it. It means our Spirit Self is receiving and He understands! Sometimes, during my meditations I find my self reading scrolls or ancient scriptures that I do not understand the meaning of, but I know that there is a part inside us which knows exactly what it means! Faith is a need. And Faith is what our daily reality is not.

"Of you, you do nothing. It is the Father/Mother within you that does it all". Let it be!

I stress again, it is important to understand and learn the *Law of Vibrations,* monitoring all of our thoughts, emotions, words and actions, because through them the fallen hierarchies have the power to feed on our Light and decrease our vibrations. It is the aim of the forces of darkness to do so and they use thoughts, emotions, words and actions to take the Light from us. When negativities, or past experiences have come to me, I have acknowledged them, blessed them, and released them into the Light. If they are so strong that they cannot be released, I asked for help! I learnt not to hang on to them. It is again the purpose of the false gods and rulers to drag us down in conflicts!

"His followers said to him 'When will the kingdom come?' He answered: It will not come by watching for it. It will not be said, Look, here it is, or look there it is. Rather, the father's kingdom is spread out upon the earth, and people do not see it."
Saying 113 – Nag Hammadi Scriptures Gospel of Thomas by Marvin Meyer (2007).

This is when our soul starts the arduous journey for purification, with repentances, and pleas to be saved. But saved from who?
Our three lower bodies of the nine, - Physical, Emotional and Mental - they indwell on Earth in our three-dimensional reality and are influenced by the outer forces of darkness which control us through another inner lower vibration - counterfeiter, our ego or lower selves - implanted in us before embodiment, and his duty is to chain us with iniquities through fear, selfish, jealousy, anger, poverty, greed, lust etc. through these our daily decisions making is manipulated, he makes us to "sin" or make wrong decisions, in order we stay in a lower vibration state of mind.

"When you make the two into one, and when you make the inner like the outer and the outer like the inner, and the upper like the lower, and when you make male and female into a single one, so that the male will not be male nor the female be female, when you make eyes in place of an eye, a hand in place of a hand, a foot in place of a foot, an image in place of an image, then you will enter the kingdom"
Saying 22:4,7 – Nag Hammadi Scriptures Gospel of Thomas by Marvin Meyer (2007).

Before the time of the ministry of Jesus the baptism was introduced with water for the purification of the sins.

"John answered them all, I baptise you with water. But one more powerful than I will come, the thongs of whose sandals I am not worthy to untie. He will baptise you with the Holy Spirit and fire." Luke 3:16-17

But it was only when Jesus Christ ascended that the Baptisms with the Holy Spirit became possible. It was purification with Fire and Light.

"I have thrown fire upon the world, and look, I am watching it until it blazes." Saying 10 – Nag Hammadi Scriptures Gospel of Thomas by Marvin Meyer (2007).

It was the job of the disciples, apostles and saints, to perform the mystery of the baptism, together spreading the Word and Faith to the rest of the world, after the ascension of Jesus Christ into the heavens.

"On one occasion, while he was eating with them, he gave them this commandment – Do not leave Jerusalem, but wait for the gift my Father promised, which you have heard me speak about, for John baptised with water, but in few days you will be baptised with the Holy Spirit." Acts 1:4-5 Holy Bible.

When the Holy Spirit descended on them, they were empowered with what they needed in order to accomplish their mission on Earth. And when they baptised, it was the Holy Spirit running through them that was going into people, realising them from their sin with fire and delivering into them what we call Spiritual Gifts!

"Now, therefore, he who shall receive the mysteries of the baptisms, then the mystery of them becometh a great, exceedingly violent, wise fire and it burneth up the sins and entereth into the soul secretly and consumeth all the sins which the counterfeiting spirit hath made fast on to it. And when it hath finished purifying all the sins which the counterfeiting spirit hath made fast on to the soul, it entereth into the body secretly and pursueth all the pursuers secretly and separateth them off on the side of the portion of the body. For it pursueth the counterfeiting spirit and the destiny and seperateth them

off from the power and from the soul and putteth them on the side of the body, so that it separateth off the counterfeiting spirit and the destiny and the body into a portion; the soul and power on the other hand it separateth into another." Third Book Page. 249 Chapter 115:300 Pistis Sophia by G.R.S Mead (1984).

And also it has been written:

> *"Jesus said: Perhaps People think I have came to impose*
> *Peace upon the world. They do not know that I have come to impose conflicts upon the earth: fire, sword, war. For there will be five in the house: there will be three against two and two against three. Father against son and son against father and they will stand alone. "*
> *Saying 16 – Nag Hammadi Scriptures Gospel of Thomas by Marvin Meyer (2007), Luke 12:52 Holy Bible.*

Who are the Two? And who are the Three? The Two are the Soul and Spirit, and after the baptism, the fight against the body, lower self and fate, which according to Pistis Sophia Gnosis, have been bound into us since our embodiment on Earth.

The Three bind us in a world of limitation which are encoded in our chakras or seals. They are the ones who, together with the fallen hierarchies, have decided our fate before we are born in this world. We need to break the chain and the binding of these seals, to release ourselves from the sins and to understand who we really are!

Once we master control of our lower bodies (physical, emotional and mental) the Higher Self or the 'Overself has a tighter grip on us, and can guide us toward what is best for us. By increasing our electrons speed, we know we are in the way to indwell with Light.

From this point on it is all about using Faith by following the inner guidance to reach Wisdom, and by then using then the Wisdom, we activate our inner Tree of Life (microcosms) with the outer Tree of Life (macrocosms) completing the Five Trees. Thereafter new Seals will be released for us, but this time they will come from the Heights.

It is through meditation that we sacrifice ourselves. For me by giving Praise and singing the Sacred Names we give the glories to the Heights. This is the curriculum to purify ourselves with Love and Light and unbinding ourselves from death.

When the perishable has been clothed with the imperishable, and the mortal with immortality, then the saying that i written will come true: "Death has been swallowed up in victory.
Where, O death, is your victory?
Where, O death, is your sting?
1 Corinthians 15:54-55 Holy Bible

Victory
Rejoice, o companions,
because the old serpent has been bound.

Virtues
Praise to you Christ, King of the angels!
O God, who are you,
who held this great consultation in your very self,
which destroyed the infernal water-drawers
with the publicans and sinners,
Who now shines in the celestial goodness?
Whence, o King, praise be to you!
O all powerful God,
from you the fountain flows with fiery love;
lead your children into the wind favourable
for the sailing of the waters
so that we also may lead them by this means
into the celestial Jerusalem.
Hildegard Von Bingen's Mystical Visions page. 382-389
Vision Thirteen (1995)

Seeking of Adam

Man, the banished Adam, seeks to pass the outer court of the Sanctuary (the exterior universe) into the sanctorum, but before him rises a vast creature armed with a flashing sword that, moving slowly but continually, sweep clear a wide circle, and through this "Ring Pass Not" the Adamic man cannot break.

The cherubim address the seeker thus: "Man, thou art dust and to dust thou shalt return. Thou wert fashioned by the Builder of Forms; thou belongest to the sphere of form, and the breath that was breathed into soul was breath of form and like a flame it shall flicker out. More than thou canst not be. Thou art a denizen of the outer world and it is forbidden thee to enter this inner place."

And the Adam replies: "Many times have I stood within this courtyard and begged admission to the Father's house and thou hast refused it me and sent me back to wander in darkness. True it is that I was fashioned out of dirt and that my Maker could not confer upon me the boom of immortality. But no more shalt thou send me away; for, wandering in the darkness, I have discovered that the Almighty hath decreed my salvation because He hath sent out of the hidden Mystery His Only Begotten who didst take upon Himself the world fashioned by the Demiurgus. Upon the elements of the world was He crucified and from Him hath poured forth the blood of my salvation. And God, entering into His creation, hath quickened it and established therein a road that leadeth to Himself. While my Maker could not give me immortality, immortality was inherent in the very dust of which I was composed, for before the world was fabricated and before the Demiurgus became the Regent of Nature the Eternal Life had impressed itself upon the face of Cosmos. This is its sign-the Cross. Do you now deny me entrance, I who have at last learned the mystery of myself?

And the voice replies: " He who is aware, IS! Behold!
Gazing about him, Adam finds himself in a radiant place, in the midst of which stands a tree with flashing jewels for fruit and entwined about its trunk a flaming, winged serpent crowned with diadem of stars. It was the voice of the serpent that had spoken.

Who art thou? Demands the Adam.

"I" the serpent answers, "am Satan who was stoned; I am the Adversary - The Lord who is against you, the one who pleads for your destruction before the Eternal Tribunal. I was your enemy upon the day that you were formed; I have led you into temptation; I have delivered you into the hands of evil; I have maligned you; I have striven ever to achieve your undoing. I am the guardian of the Tree of knowledge and I have sworn that none whom I can lead astray shall partake of its fruits"

The Adam replies: "For uncounted ages have I been thy servant. In my ignorance I listened to thy words and led me into paths of sorrow. Thou hast placed in my mind dreams of power, and when I struggled to realize those dreams they brought me naught but pain. Thou hast sowed in me the seeds of desire, and when I lusted after the things of the flesh agony was my only recompense. Thou hast sent me false prophets and false reasoning, and when I strove to grasp the magnitude of Truth I found thy laws were false and only dismay rewarded my strivings. I am done with thee forever, O artfulSpirit! I have tired of thy world of illusions. No longer will I labor in thy vineyards of iniquity. Get thee behind me, tempter, and the host of thy temptations. There is no happiness, no peace, no good, no future in the doctrines of selfishness, hate, and passion preached by thee. All these things do I cast aside. Renounced is thy rule forever!

And the serpent answer: "Behold, O Adam, the nature of thy Adversary!" The serpent disappears in a blinding sunburst of radiance and in its place stands an angel resplendent in shining, golden garments with great scarlet wings that spread from one corner of the heavens to the other. Dismayed and awestruck, the Adam falls before the Divine Creature. " I am the Lord who is against thee and thus accomplishes thy salvation,"
continues the voice. "Thou hast hated me, but through the ages yet to be thou shalt bless me, for I have led thee out of the sphere of the Demiurgus; I have turned thee against the illusion of worldliness; I have weaned thee of desire; I have awakened in thou soul the immortality of which I myself partake. Follow me, O Adam, for I am

the Way, the Life, and the Truth!"
The forgotten books, The Teachings of All Ages by Manly P. Hall, pages 378-380
Republished 2008 by Forgotten Books

Conclusion

We are close to a major turning point and the opening of the new book! From my very first vision I understood the power of Christ is real and active in all of humanity and He really saved us.

Reading the *Nag Hammadi Scriptures* revealed to me many other mysteries, for within them lie many gospels and rituals that for me, have been written by Luminaries for the benefit of humanity or at least for some of humanity to acknowledge as we all have the same opportunity and it is driven by the free will God gave us! I believe, all humanity will regain our lost memory when the last seal is opened, releasing all past records from the Great Pyramid of Giza. This can happen only when the right individuals team up to work together and safely open this sacred vault, before the memory of humanity will be erased once again.

There are a multitude of secrets many secrets to be unveiled and many are difficult to digest for us because we have been indoctrinated and made slaves by them. We have become drunk and blind, cloaked by a thick veil that separates our minds and covers our heart from the higher truths!

"But their minds were made dull, for to this day the same veil remains when the old covenant is read. It has not been removed, because only in Christ is it taken away." 2 Corinthians 3:14 Holy Bible.

The existence of these veils is real and they are encoded into letters, words and in our consciousess. Only by wearing the Garment of Light – Christ –

can we understand the real meaning of it!

Until now most of the people in the world are not sure why Jesus Christ was killed, as well as disciples and saints.

"Jesus said to his followers, compare me to something and tell me what I am like.
Simon Peter said to him, you are like a righteous messenger.
Matthew said to him, you are like a wise philosopher.
Thomas said to him, Teacher, my mouth is utterly unable to say what you are like.
Jesus said, I am not your teacher, because you have drunk, you have become
intoxicated from the bubbling spring that I have tended.
And he took him, and withdrew, and spoke three sayings to him.
When Thomas came back to his friends, they asked him, what did Jesus say to you?
Thomas said to them, If I tell you one of the sayings he spoke to me, you will pick
up rocks and stone me, and the fire will come from the rocks and consume you."
Saying 13 – Nag Hammadi Scriptures Gospel of Thomas by Marvin Meyer
(2007).

Jesus brought truths to us and the rulers (archons) did not like that these truths were going to be revealed to all of humanity!

"Jesus said, seek and you will find. In the past, however, I did not tell you the things
about which you asked me then. Now I am willing to tell them, but you are not
seeking them."
Saying 92 – Nag Hammadi Scriptures Gospel of Thomas by Marvin Meyer
(2007).

He brought these truths to save us!

"How miserable is the body that depends on a body, and how miserable is the soul
that depends on these two."
Saying 87 – Nag Hammadi Scriptures Gospel of Thomas by Marvin Meyer
(2007).

And He left His Words for us to find the ways to the truths!

"He gave them [who had followed Him] laws and delivered unto them commandments, saying: Keep my sayings and I will give unto you eternal life; I will send Powers unto you, yea, I will strengthen you with mighty spirits, and will give unto you the dominion of the desire: no one shall hinder your will, and you shall bring forth aeons, worlds, and heavens. When the intellectual spirits come to dwell in you then shall ye become gods, then shall ye know that ye came forth from God and shall ye behold Him within yourselves, in your eternities shall He dwell." Page. 70 the Brucianus Codex Gnosis of Light by F. Lamplugh and R.A. Gilbert

And it is all written; one needs only to seek to find and embrace Faith, He showed us who are our enemies.

"Blessings on the person who knows at what point the robbers are going to enter, so that he may arise, bring together his estate and arm himself before they enter." Saying 103 – Nag Hammadi Scriptures Gospel of Thomas by Marvin Meyer (2007).

But, also, he sacrificed himself for us to purify our sins!

"Just as man is destined to die once, and after that to face judgement, so Christ was sacrificed once to take away the sins of many people; and he will appear a second time, not to bear sin, but to bring salvation to those who are waiting for him." Hebrew 9:27-28. Holy Bible.

From my personal experience, I understand how difficult it is to keep our minds open, because we are being bombarded from every direction but it is for this reason he gave Faith and Prayers so that we may ask for help if we want to be helped because on our own we are helpless.

"There was a rich person who had a great deal of money. He said, I shall invest my money so that I may sow, reap, plant and fill my storehouse with produce, that I may lack nothing. These were the things he was thinking in his heart, but that very night he died. Whoever has ears should hear." Saying 63 – Nag Hammadi Scriptures Gospel of Thomas by Marvin Meyer

(2007).

We must try to find time to connect with our higher sources, and question daily the true reasons for our existence on earth.

"If you do not fast from the world, you will not find the Kingdom. If you do not observe the Sabbath as a Sabbath, you will not see the father."
Saying 27 — Nag Hammadi Scriptures Gospel of Thomas by Marvin Meyer
(2007).

Maybe the purpose of this book — *Bring to the Light* — is to unveil the mysteries behind His sayings and parables because, even after two thousand years, most of us do not understand what He was trying to tell us.

"The harvest is large but the workers are few. So beg the master to send out workers to the harvest."
Saying 73 — Nag Hammadi Scriptures Gospel of Thomas by Marvin Meyer
(2007).

In this Age, many are searching to find their answers and there is an explosion of spirituality all around the globe. I believe this is telling us something, time is close for the fulfilment of the promises made thousand years ago.

"Someone said, Master, There are many around the drinking trough, but there is nothing in the well."
Saying 74 — Nag Hammadi Scriptures Gospel of Thomas by Marvin Meyer
(2007).

There is an old prophesy that says that many will be deceived by the false, and I believe this is the time to start to be vigilant, and to decide who we follow. When we under·;and the truths, we will understand that they are the same as they were two thousand years ago!

"Grapes are not harvested from thorn bushes, nor are figs gathered from thistles, for they yield no fruit. A good person brings forth good from the storehouse, a bad person brings forth evil things from the corrupt storehouse in the heart and says evil things. For from abundance of the heart this person brings forth evil things."
Saying 45 – Nag Hammadi Scriptures Gospel of Thomas by Marvin Meyer
(2007).

A new world is ready to replace the old,

"A world made he, an aeon, a town; the world which is called 'Incorruptibility' and 'Jerusalem'. It is also called 'New Earth' and 'Self perfect' and 'Without King'. This Earth is an earth that brings forth gods, a life-giving earth indeed".
Page. 53-54 The Gnosis of Light – A Translation of the Untitled Apocalypse contained in the Brucianus Codex by F Lampugh and R.A. Gilbert (2006).

This is the Age of transformation and transmutation, the Age of the Holy Spirit. The most important thing for us to understand and acknowledge is the role of our Divine Mother, that little has been written about and, for thousands of years, the rulers have tried to suppress Her power. In truth, it is because of the will of the Divine Mother that Christ was sent to Earth. She is the Creator force. She is who encompasses everything and everywhere. On many different levels, She is represented by the Holy Spirit, She is Mind, She is all the Universes encompassing everything, She manifests Herself in Sophia (Wisdom), in Mother Earth and also in our souls and matter. Her essence is in our feminine side. At the Highest levels Christ is within Her and so is the Father. In the lower levels she need to be restored and re-connected with the Heights and through Sophia and Christ we will know the Glory of the Father.

If we look at how the females are treated today in our modern world, in many cultures and religions, females are considered vastly inferior to men and are not awarded even basic rights within their societies. People need to understand that, as humans, we are all sons and daughters of Eve and through her, humanity exists! On the spiritual level it is our Divine Mother that manifested all creations through Her Son "Christ". being Mind and Thought. Through the Divine Mother, Christ performs His powers and in Christ we find the Glory of the Father!

"Whoever blasphemes against the Father will be forgiven, and whoever blasphemes against the Son will be forgiven, but whoever blasphemes against the Holy Spirit will not be forgiven, either on Earth or in Heaven."
Saying 44 – Nag Hammadi Scriptures Gospel of Thomas by Marvin Meyer (2007).

And also
"Whoever does not hate father and mother as I do cannot be a follower of me, and whoever does not love Father and Mother as I do cannot be a follower of me. For my mother gave me falsehood, but my true Mother gave me life."
Saying 101 – Nag Hammadi Scriptures Gospel of Thomas by Marvin Meyer (2007).

The fallen hierarchy understood this since the beginning, which is why they have been trying to suppress Her power; they have corrupted and contaminated her by using her creative powers for creating limitations!

This feminine power is within each one of us; it is the receiving force that synthesises everything and needs to be uncovered and nurtured. It is the part of us that allows the Light to enter into our body. So if she is the starter to connect with the Light, the masculine is the end, the accomplishment. Oneness is reached with the peace between these two forces, when balance is achieved.

"When you make two into one, you will become children of humanity, and when you say, Mountain, move from here, it will move, or if two make peace in the single house, they will say to the mountain, move from here and it will move."
Saying 106 – Nag Hammadi Scriptures Gospel of Thomas by Marvin Meyer (2007).

I believe humanity in these coming years will experience many new wonders;

some of which will deceive and lead us astray, and others will help us. It is foolish to think, if one is blessed with the knowledge, or because he is a follower of a group, organization or religion, he will be granted Wisdom and Glories.

Now Jesus heard the twelve dispute among themselves. The spirit of the carnal self was
moving in their hearts, they were questioning amongs themselves who was the greatest
in the sight of God and man. And Jesus said, You men, for shame! the greatest is the
servant of the rest. And then he called to him a little child; he took it in his arms ans
said - The greatest is the little child, and if you would be great at all you must become
as is this child innocence, in truth, in purity in life. Great men scorn not little things of
earth; he who regards and honors such a child, regards and honors me, and he who
scorns a child, scorn me.
If you would enter through the kingdom gate you must be humble as this little child.
The Aquarian Gospel of Jesus Christ (1911), Section xvii, Chapter 131:8-12

Many do believe they are "the way", and this thinking has hardened their hearts with arrogance *(The Law of Relativity, The Universal Laws)*! We indwell with death and Light and until death is eliminated, we all fight together with Faith, Wisdom and Love. **And don't be fooled. Nobody knows exactly when the New will take place and the Old will end!**

Ages to comes shall revival of wisdom to those who shall inherit thy place on this star.
They shall, in turn, come into wisdom and learn to banish the darkness by Light. Yet
greatly must they strive through the ages to bring unto themselves the freedom of
Light. Many who are bound in darkness shall strive to hold others from the Light.
Then shall there come unto man the great warfare that shall make the Earth tremble
and shake in its course.
Aye, then shall the Dark Brothers open the warfare between Light and the night.
When man again shall conquer the ocean and fly in the air on wings like birds; when
he has learned to harness the lighting, then shall the time of warfare begin. Great shall
the battle be twixt the forces, great the warfare of darkness and Light. Nation shall rise
against nation using the dark forces to shatter the Earth. Weapons of force shall wipe

out the Earth-men until half of the races of men shall be gone. Then shall come forth the Sons of the Morning and give their edict to the children of men, saying:

"O men, cease from thy striving against thy brother. Only thus can ye come to the Light. Cease from thy unbelief, O my brother, and follow the path and know ye are right." *Page 67, The Law of Cause and Effect & The Key of Prophecy, The Emerald Tablet Of Thoth The Atlantean, Translation and interpretation by Doreal*

"For the Word of God is living and active. Sharper than any double-edged sword, it penetrates even to dividing soul and spirit, joints and marrow; it judge the thoughts and attitudes of the heart. Nothing in all creation is hidden from God's sight. Everything is uncovered and laid bare before the eyes of him to whom we must give account." Hebrew 4:12-13 Holy Bible

There are difficult times ahead and everyone is already feeling the pressures I starts in the microcosms within ourselves and expands through out the macrocosms of our struggles, arguments and disease within families, friends, cities, countries, Mother Earth and Heavens as we are all interconnected. Only with the power of Love and Light we can save this sinking ship.

I hope from my heart that this book has delivered the message it was meant to deliver. I conclude with this:

"At that time if anyone says to you, 'look, here is the Christ! Or, there he is! Do not believe it.

For false Christ and false prophets will appear and perform great signs and miracles to deceive even the elect − if that were possible.

See, I have told you ahead of time.

So if anyone tells you, there he is, out in the desert, do not go out, or Here he is, in the inner rooms, do not believe it. For as lightning that comes from the east is visible even in the west, so will be the coming of the Son of Man. Wherever there is a carcass, there the vultures will gather. Immediately after the distress of those days

The sun will be darkened, and the moon will not give its light;

The stars will fall from the sky, and the heavenly bodies will be shaken.

At that time the sign of the Son of Man will appear in the sky, and all the nations of the earth will mourn. They will see the Son of Man coming on the clouds of the sky, with the power of great glory. And he will send his angels with a loud trumpet call, and they will gather his elect from the four winds, from one end of the heavens to the other." Matthew 24:23-31 Holy Bible.

In Christ with Love, Amen

Thanksgiving

We thank you
Every soul and heart reaches out to you,
O name free of trouble,
honored with the designation God,
Praised with the designation Father.
To all and all things
Come fatherly kindness and affection and love.
And if there is sweet and simple instruction,
It grants us mind, word and knowledge:
Mind, that we may understand you,
Word, that we may interpret you,
Knowledge that we may know you.
We are happy
Enlightened by your knowledge.
We are happy.
You have taught us about yourself.
We are happy.
While we were in the body,
You have made us divine through your knowledge.

The thanksgiving of one approaching you
Is this alone:
That we know you.
We have known you,
Light of mind.
Life of life,
We have known you.
Womb of every creature,
We have known you.
Womb pregnant with the Father's nature,

We have known you.
Eternal constancy of the Father who conceives,
So have we worshipped your goodness.
One favour we ask
We wish to be sustained in knowledge.
One protection we desire:
That we not stumble in this life.

Meyer, M. *Nag Hammadi Scriptures*, Harper Collins, New York, 2007.
Page 422-423

Illustrations

Visions and Pictographics

Prayers, Hymns and Invocations

Bibliography

Villoldo, A. *Shaman Healer Sage*, Bantam Books, London, 2000.

Villoldo, A. *Mending the Past and Healing the Future with Soul Retrieval*, Hay House, London, 2005.

Villoldo, A. *The Four Insights: Wisdom, Power, and Grace of the Earthkeepers*, Hay House, London, 2006.

Bear Heart with Molly Larkin. *The Wind Is My Mother*, Berkley Books, New York, 1998.

Milanovich, N. & McCune, S. *The Light Shall Set You Free*, Athena Publishing, Scottsdale, AZ, 1996.

Sams, J. & Carson, D. *Medicine Cards*, St Martin Press, New York, 1999.

Hurtak, J. J. *YHWH – The Book Of Knowledge: The Keys Of Enoch*, The Academy For Future Science, Los Gatos, California, 2004.

Bias Clifford. *Qabalah, Tarot & The Western Mystery Tradition, The 22 Connecting Paths on the Tree of Life*, Samuel Weiser, York Beach, Maine, 1997.

Milanovich, N.J. & Meltesen, J. *Sacred Journey To Atlantis*, Athena Publishing, Scottsdale, AZ, 1994.

Hurtak, J. J. *The Seventy Two Living Divine Names of the Most High*, The Academy For Future Science, Los Gatos, California, 2009.

Vaughan, S. *Kinangiology*, O Book, Ropley UK, 2009.

Milanovich, N.J., Rice, B. and Ploski C. *We, The Arthurians*, Athena Publishing, Scottsdale, AZ, 1990.

Gewurz, E. *The Qabalah: The Feminine Elements in Man and Their Redeeming Power*, Kessinger Publishing.

Gewurs, E. *The Mysteries Of The Qabalah, Volume 2*, The Yogi Publication Society, Chicago, 1922.

Vincent, S. K. *The English Qabalah*, 8TH House Publishing, Montreal, 2008.

Bailey, A. A. *From Intellect to Intuition*, Lucis Press Ltd, New York, 2003.

Levi, Dowling E. S. *The Aquarian Gospel Of Jesus The Christ*, E.S. Dowling, Los Angeles, 1911.

Thomas, T. *Units 12-13 Sikhism: The Voice of the Guru*, The Open University Press, Milton Keynes, 1981.

Roman, S. & Packer, D. *Opening To Channel, How to connect with Your Guide*, H J Kramer, Tiburon, 1987.

Selby, J. *Kundalini Awakening*, Bantam Books, New York, 1992.

Mead, G.R.P. *Pistis Sophia Agnostic Gospel*, Spiritual Science Library, Blauvelt, 1984.

Hurtak, J. J. & Hurtak, D. *Pistis Sophia: A Coptic Text of Gnosis with Commentary*, The Academy For Future Science, Los Gatos, California, 2003.

Hurtak, J. J. & Hurtak, D. *The Gospel of Mary: A Text of Mary Magdalene with Commentary*, The Academy For Future Science, Los Gatos, California, 2008.

Vermes, G., The Complete Dead Sea Scrolls in English Revised Edition, Penguin Books, London, 2004.

Meyer, M. *Nag Hammadi Scriptures*, Harper Collins, New York, 2007.

Von Bingen's, H. *Mystical Visions*, Bear & Company, Rochester, 1986.

Hurtak, J. J. & Hurtak, D. *The Five Bodies,*, The Academy For Future Science, Los Gatos, California, 1994.

Meyer, M. *Gospel of Thomas*, Harper Collins, New York, 1992.

Manly, P Hall, *The Teaching of All Ages*, The forgotten books, Republished 2008 by Forgotten Books

Doreal, *The Emerald Tables of Thoth The Atlantean Translation and Interpretation by Doreal*, Revised edition 2006, Colorado USA

If you have any questions regarding this book please contact:
info@bringtothelight.co.uk
www.bringtothelight.co.uk